THE EARLY DAYS OF NOTTINGHAM FOREST

WRITTEN AND PUT TOGETHER

BY

RON CLARKE

TO

GRAHAM

BEST WISHES

FROM

Ron Clarke

First published in December 2011

Pictures from Ron Clarke's personal collection
Steve Nicholson (Derby Telegraph)
Nottingham Forest Football Club
Laurence Rampling (West Bromich Albion F.C.)
Joanne & Gary Clarke

Published by Ron Clarke

FOREWORD

This is a truly remarkable collection of Nottingham Forest memborabilia Ron and Paul have collected over the years.

What is even more impressive is how diverse and wide-ranging the images and statistics are.

The majority of the contents of this book have previously never been seen and never before has so much been presented together in one place.

A well deserved congratulations to Ron the end result is a fascinating book whieh is an interesting read and a real must have, for all true Forest fans.

Paul McKenna
(Former Nottingham Forest Captain)

The readers of this book will see it's taken a lot of time and hard work to put together, we believe that some of the content may never have been seen before.

The match reports are taken from actual newspaper cuttings of the year and amongst the photos, which are pretty rare, there are some images that have never been seen in any book to date.

There are the views of the game, seen through the eyes of the late and famous Tinsley Lindley, who we think is the youngest ever player to play for Nottingham Forest at the tender age of just 16 years and 112 days old who scored 3 goals on his first team debut against the Wolverhampton Stafford Roadworks on February 17th 1882, he had previously scored a record 85 goals in one season for the Nottingham Forest second eleven and 3 years later when at Cambridge scoring 59 goals in 46 matches.

Included in the match reports is the complete report of the Wednesbury National Charity Cup Final, in which Forest won to take home their first ever cup, also a complete report of the 1898 English Cup Final against Derby County.

There is also a "Oxo" fixture card with a photo of the Forest team on it for the 1911-1912 season, it could be that Oxo were Nottingham Forest's first sponsor.

Read on and hopefully enjoy the book.

CONTENTS

Nottingham Forest Inside Notes
and some through the eyes of
Tinsley Lindley
and
Nottingham Forest Match Reports

It is just as well to call a club by the name which its original founders selected, therefore let us promptly point out on the common errors of the football world, this organisation is not Notts Forest but Nottingham Forest, The former is a popular corruption of the Foresters and has never claimed any connection with the County. Ancient and honourable associations are linked with the Reds and whatever may be said of the club, none should describe it as of mushroom origin. Indeed with perhaps the single exception of Stoke, Nottingham Forest were established before any of the leaguers, the historic town of Nottingham was one of those centres where football flourished, before the great development of the game, only Cambridge, Sheffield and London had clubs before Nottingham.

In 1860 there was quite a football boom in the cutlery metropolis. In matters of sport there has always been intense rivalry between the neighbouring industrial hives, Nottingham and shire town made converts in the capital of the lace trade in the sixties, clubs were formed in Nottingham and amongst them the Forest which still exists. Despite a somewhat chequered career, the late 70s found them at the zenith of their fame, the mid 80s witnessed their decline and the 90s have watched their restoration, if not their pristine powers, at least to a most honourable position among the leading teams of the country.

But let us not hark back to 1865 which seems to be generally agreed upon as the date of foundation. A number of young men had for several years played a game called Shinny which was a crude kind of hockey. They disported themselves on the great public recreation ground known as the Forest, this had been a racecourse, prior to the utilisation of Colwick Park for that purpose, and a large tract of open ground on which was played the great cricket matches when the game was fought for 50 or 100 guineas a side and when the contestants figured in the chimney pot hats, which old prints have rendered familiar to us.

The famous William Howitt has left us a grand word-painting of one of these battles, in which he describes the Forest, (The trees of Sherwood once embedded their roots there), as a long furzy common crowned on the top by about 20 windmills and descending in a steep slope to a fine level ground, which the racecourse runs. It gave good William Howitt a vivid idea of an amphitheatre and it was, then on this famous trusting mean of sportsmen that these young men played "Shinny" on Saturday afternoons on the ground immediately east of the grand stand and paddock enclosure. The suggestion that the shinny men should take up football was not at first received with favour, but an open air meeting of about 15 players the subject was debated. Finally a Mr. J. S. Scrimshaw was asked to summon the members to the Clinton Arms hostelry about a mile from the ground to settle the question. The gathering agreed to form the Forest Football Club, among those who were members of the shinny club and who, sooner or later adopted football and must thus be looked upon as the founders of the organisation were, - A. Barks, W. Brown, P. Brown, C. F. Daft, T. Gamble, T. G. Howitt, W. L. Hussey, W. R. Lymberry, P. Hawley.

NOTTINGHAM FOREST GROUNDS

1879 - Meadows Ground
1880 - Trent Bridge Ground
1882 - Parkside Ground, Lenton
1885 - Gregory Ground
1890 - Town Ground

TINSLEY LINDLEY

He was the youngest ever player to play for Nottingham Forest at the tender age of just 16 years 112 days old, he made his debut against Wolverhampton Stafford Roadworks on February 17th 1882, scoring 3 goals, Forest winning by 6 goals to 0, the following week against Wolverhampton, again scoring 3 goals Forest winning by 6 goals to 0.

He also holds the record of scoring 85 goals in one season for the Forest in 1881 - 1882 3 years later when at Cambridge scoring 59 goals in 46 matches.

1881 NOTTINGHAM FOREST FOOTBALL CLUB

Headquarters:

Club Room, Maypole Yard, Off Clumber Street, Nottingham.

There were about 130 members

President:	W. E. Denison
Secretary:	W. R. Lymberry
Weekday Cross, Ass, Sec.	T. G. Howitt

Committee meetings Friday Evenings at 7pm

SOME HISTORY OF NOTTINGHAM FOREST

Nottingham Forest Football Club was founded in 1865 by a body of young fellows, who had for several years utilised the forest as a great public recreation ground or the purpose of the game, which was locally termed "Shinny". But most parts of England and throughout Scotland, the game was known as Shinty, as was the original form of the new elaborated pastime of hockey. When the boom of football in Sheffield came about the contagion naturally soon spread to Nottingham and those young fellows debated as to whether they should patronise servatire and there was some opposition to the suggestion that a football team should be started, finally one of their number, J. S. Scrimshaw, called a meeting of the fraternity at the Clinton Arms Hotel in Nottingham, where the Nottingham Forest Football Club was formed, the matter having previously been debated at an open air meeting attended by about 15 players.

RED SHIRTS

From Charlie Daft, the elder brother of Richard Daft, a dozen red flannel caps were purchased and to this day red has been the clubs only wear. Who is not familiar with their garabaldi shirts? It is worthy to note, that a few old foresters were the founders of the Woolwich Arsenal team who adopted the same scarlet banner for a couple of years after the football section had been formed.

"Shinny" was indulged in as well, but it was apparent that before long that in order to have a vigorous club, it would be necessary for one of the sections to be abandoned, the shinny men were finally outvoted and the Nottingham Forest Football Club then became the full title. The rules were a great mixture of the Rugby code and the different laws recognised by the London and Sheffield Associations indeed there was so little uniformity of play in those days that matches were generally decided under the rules of the club on whose ground the battle was fought, not infrequently the first half of a contest was decided under one code and the second half under another. The description of the only goal which a match between Nottingham Forest and Notts County produced in 1866 is suggestive of the handling, rather than the dribbling code, we are told that the clubs fought away all afternoon, but nothing tangible was scored until close to the call of time, when there was a sort of a steeplechase across the goal line, and over the railings near the grandstand between a player named "Hugh Brown" of Notts and W. Revis of the Forest, the latter touched down the ball, and a place kick was taken 15 yards at right angles to the goal line. Being successful, the Forest were proclaimed the winners, there was no cross bar, the ball had merely to go between the posts.

SHINGUARD PIONEERS

In 1868, a good friend of the reds, Mr. W. R. Lymberry took office as honourary secretary, he proved an enthusiastic worker and the club went ahead rapidly. It is worthy to note that the Forest were responsible for the football shinguard, this was the idea of S. W. Widdowson who registered it and brought it out in 1874. It was during one of the thrilling contests between Forest and Sheffield Norfolk that the referees whistle was introduced, this was first used on the Forest ground in 1878. The Forest were perfecting their football too and they learned much from the famous engineers who undertook the first football tour in history, and by their methodical ways did much to show the value of combination. Towards the end of the 1870s the Forest eleven had a peculiar formation, they had a goalkeeper, 2 backs, 1 half back, 2 three quarter backs and 5 forwards. The Notts Castle club was dissolved in 1878 and most of the leading members joined the Forest, the latter became very strong, they first entered the F.A. Cup competition in 1878 - 1879, beating Notts County by 3 goals to 1, with a team composed of.

A. Sands

C. J, Caborn   E. Luntley

A. J. Bates   S. W. Widdowson   A. M. Holroyd

A. Smith   A. Goodyer   J. Turner   P. Earp   W. Luntley

of these players 4 were capped

A. Sands   Widdowson   Luntley   Goodyer

Another distinction claimed by Forest was that they played in the only F.A. Cup Semi-Final that has ever been played in Scotland, they drew at Derby against Queens Park, 1 - 1, and replayed at Merchiston Park, Edinburgh, which Forest lost by 3 goals to 0.

ONE CUP VICTORY

When the professional era arrived, the Forest refusing to march with the times deteriated rapidly. But in 1889, Mr. Harry Radford took over the duties of secretary and insisted on the club being conducted on up-to-date lines. For the season of 1890-1891, professionals were engaged, and they made fairly rapid headway, heading the alliance in 1891-1892 and were made members of the league in the following season. It was not until the season of 1897-1898, that the Forest succeeded in winning the English Cup under the leadership of that magnificent half-back Frank Forman, they beat Derby County at Crystal Palace by 3 goals to 1 with a team that consisted of:

D. Allsop, G. H. Richards, A. Scott, F. Forman, J. McPherson, W. Wragg, T. McInnes, A. Richie, L. Benbow, A. Capes and A. Spouncer.

This was the only occasion Forest have reached the last round, though they figured in no less than 8 semi-finals of the English cup, the only other cup they have won was in 1882/1883 season by beating West Bromwich Albion by 5 goals to 3 for the Wednesbury National Charity Cup, which they took back to the Maypole Yard, Club H.Q. in Nottingham.

The Forest have never been without high first class players, they have had 2 goalkeepers who have played for England in Harry Linacre and Sam Hardy and J. Hanna who was capped by Ireland, Linacre stood 6ft high and was a nephew of Frank and Fred Forman, and like his uncles was born in the village of Aston-on-Trent. In 1905 he played against Scotland and Wales Hardy's transfer from Aston Villa for £1,000 in 1921 created no little surprise, and he helped the club win promotion in his first season.

Allsop who helped the club win the cup was a Derby man, his previous club was Derby Junction.

The Forest developed another fine goalkeeper in Len Langford a Rossington man who went on to play for Manchester City.

Ritchie and Scott the cup final backs were a grand pair in harness and Scott particularly won great popularity by his skill and loyalty to the club. A brother of John Scott who made a name with Sunderland, he joined the reds at the age of 20 years in 1890/09 season from Coatbridge Albion Rovers, he has merely gained junior honours and though standing only 5ft high he was for his inches one of the finest backs the club has ever employed. C. T. Craig a dundoian later challenged comparison with Ritchie, he was a splendidly built fellow, a sure kick resolute tackler, and he also was scrupulously fair. He was just as clever with head as well has feet and had the priceless virtue of pulling out his best when his side needed it.

Sam Hardy - Prince of Goalkeepers

FINE BACKS

James Iremonger was another grand Forest back who in 1901 was in England's team against the Scots and a year later against Ireland. Although Yorkshire born he lived most of his life in Nottingham and became a successful Nottingham Cricketer. He could play on either side, other capable defenders who have worn the red jersey were J. W. White (Iremongers partner) who afterwards went to New Brompton, W. McCurdy (previously with the Vale of Clyde and Luton). H. M. Bulling (from Watford) and T. Gibson (who was useful at centre forward). My choice of the best half back's in the Forest service is Frank Forman, J. McPherson and G. Henderson, Forman who joined the club from Derby County, upon who's league list he had remained for some time without obtaining the opportunities to which his exceptional abilities justly entitled him. He was a perfect glutton for work, he had the knack of being here there and everywhere, although he could never be charged with indiscreet wandering, he was capped 9 times by England. And a complete master of half-back tactics, he was at home anywhere and delighted to shoot goals from long range and from the spot.

J. McPherson a centre half and a born captain came from Motherwell and had the unique distinction of holding both F.A. and Scottish Cup medals, in addition to 2 international caps, 7 inter county caps and a rare collection of medals, when he retired Frank Forman became centre half.

George Henderson a Burnbank product who was with the Airdrieonians in 1895 and assisted Preston North End, Swindon Town and Millwall before settling with the Forest was an exceedingly capable left back. So was W. Wragg, R. Norris (who's career was blighted by a fractured leg sustained while playing with Aston Villa) and R. S. Wallace.

Now Tom Graham who has played back, half-back and centre forward for the club is being talked of as England's future pivitt.

Fred Norman and elder brother of Frank was England's outside left against all 3 countries in 1899, he joined Forest in 1894 from Derby County whom he had assisted as an amateur, but it was on the right wing that he did his best work for the Forest.

Tom McInnes who played for Cowlairs before and Third Lanark after joining Forest suffered a partial breakdown while with the Scottish Senior club, but Mr. David Calderhead took the risk of signing him for Lincoln City for whom he did a grand service for several seasons.

C. H. Richards who was an inside right in the Forest team that won the cup, and was capped by England against Ireland in 1898. He served both Nottingham clubs and later was with Grimsby Town and Leicester Fosse.

J. H. Derrick served Forest well in all 3 inside positions. The club has employed quite a number of grand centre forwards, Sam Widdowson, a splendid herculean player was just as good at centre half as at inside left, but the pick of the centres was Tinsley Lindley, who became a barrister, he was in the Cambridge eleven for 4 years being captain in 1888. He represented England with signal success on 13 occasions and gave useful assistance to the Corinthians.

At inside left the club have been served well by Arthur Capes, Sandy Higgins, E. G. Morris and W. Lindley, but I am inclined to A. G. Morris a Welshman who was with Aberystwyth and Swindon Town before joining the reds. He figured on 21 occasions in the Welsh team between 1906 and 1911, The Forest also found an outside left of the first flight when in 1898, they induced Gainsborough Trinity to release W. A. Spouncer who was capped by England against Wales. Sheffield United signed him first but gave him a free transfer to his old club and the Forest reaped the full benefit of his services.

HERE IS MY BEST ELEVEN

Sam Hardy

C. T. Craig A. Scott

J. McPherson

Frank Norman G, Henderson

F. Norman C. Richards T. Lindley W. Spouncer A. Morris

This side includes internationals of 3 different countries

S. Hardy T. Lindley W. Spouncer A. Morris C. Richards

Frank and Fred Normand

Centre Forward Tinsley Lindley played against Ireland in 1886, 1887, 1888 and 1891. He was captain against the Scots in 1888 in the victory of 5 goals to 0.

GAMES IN A RED SHIRT

Those who have followed the fortunes of the Forest through the years will not need to be reminded of the feats of Tinsley Lindley of the reds.

In the year of 1882 he scored 85 goals off his own boot, as many as some teams score in a season at the present day, 3 years later he put the ball in the net 59 times in 46 matches, what a centre forward and how the opposition quaked.

Not that the luck of the Nottingham scoring genius always held good, he came away from one game without a goal to his credit. One time on Wandsworth common playing against a really good team called the Swifts, a friend of his bet him a bottle of champagne he would not score, he took him on, but until 15 minutes from the end the goal held a charmed life, he hit the posts, the bar, the goalkeeper and fired over the top, it seemed impossible to score, his friend raised the bet to 2 bottles of champagne, what about 3 to 1 that I do not score twice? He was delighted "and a case to a bottle that you will not do a hat-trick" he shouted. In the last 10 minutes of that match, Tinsley Lindley netted 5 times and what a party they had in celebration. It was in March 1891 that Tinsley Lindley played his last first class match, it was at Liverpool for the Corinthians against Everton, he retired from the game that day, "Why"? he was asked, frankly it was because he had, had enough and football was not like it was. He would not go so far as to state that the advent of professionalism, but to the social distinctions which are the outcome of it.

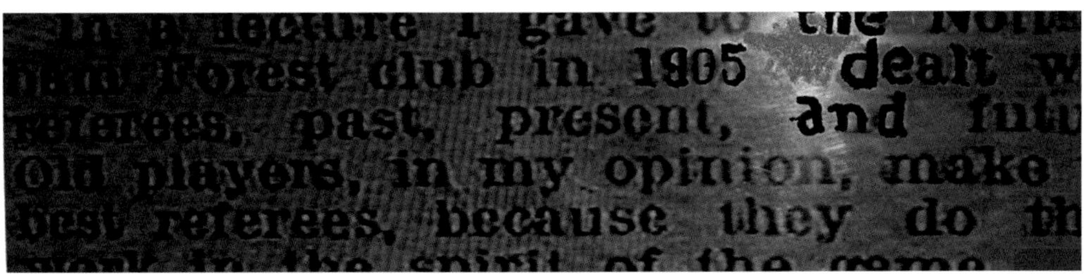
lecture I gave to the
Forest club in 1905 dealt
referees, past, present, and
Old players, in my opinion, make
best referees, because they do

VIEWS OF THE GAME TODAY

Like Mr. Parr who played for the Forest on many a Saturday afternoon, Tinsley Lindley believes that modern day football misses a great deal of the grandeur of the past. The professional forward of today is absolutely afraid to shoot, he dallies about with the ball, and when he does think it's safe to try the goalkeeper, he is so far out of practice, that he cannot score. In his day a forward never hesitated to kick hard at goal when he was anywhere within 20 yards of it, he always contested that where a modern day player puts in 3 shots we would have tried 9 or 10, and of course, we scored more goals. Then again, footballers are not allowed to charge an opponent seriously these days, infact if a forward could learn to dribble a ball backwards, he could score without interference as no one would be allowed to charge him in the back.

PLAYERS WORTH £40 A WEEK

THE FAMOUS CORINTHIANS INTERNATIONAL FOOTBALL REFORMS

by

Tinsley Lindley, March 17th 1930

13 times an international in the golden days of association football, Tinsley Lindley the famous centre forward of the Corinthians and Nottingham Forest and one of the players who helped to create the subtilties of soccer forward play and to make W. N. Cobbold the prince of dribblers.

Tinsley Lindley learned his football at the Nottingham High School, making captain, he joined Nottingham Forest when a little over 16 years old playing with some regularity for them for 2 years, in his first game for the Forest against Wolverhampton Stafford Roadworks at Stafford Road, scoring 3 goals, the following week again against Wolves scoring 3 more, he went on to study at Cambridge and secured his colours in his first year and was captain for 2 years in 1886-1887 being elected a member of the Corinthians and remained a playing member of that organisation until he retired from football in March 1891 at Liverpool, after a game against Everton.

He played his first game for the Corinthians against Blackburn Rovers on December 15th 1884, who were then the holders of the English Cup and beat them by 8 goals to 1, in our side were J. M. Rendall, who later became headmaster of Winchester, Andy Watson a Scotsman, W. F. Beardsley a Sheffield man, A. Amos, C. Holde-White, F. E. Saunders, F. W. Pawson, B. W. Spilsbury, A. J. Millar, the non-de-plume of Dr. John Smith the old Queens Park centre forward, W. N. Cobbold the prince of dribblers, and Tinsley Lindley. In the early days of the Corinthians, Cambridge players predominated and their style of play was generally adopted, it is still played by the Corinthians of today, it consists of keeping the ball under control on the ground and passing quickly and always forward to the other players while on the move.

THE CORINTHIAN WAY

At this early stage of the game, there is good deal of uncertainty with regard to the formation of a side, whether there should be 6 forwards or 5. Considerable successes were gained by Cambridge with 5 forwards and 3 half-backs instead of 2, and this led to the general adoption of the formation which has existed ever since Tinsley Lindley played his first game against Preston North End in December 1884, the North team consisted of Rose, Howarth, Nick Ross, Robertson, Ferguson, Dewhurst, Graham, Gordon , Goodall, Thomson, and Drummond. Guess who the linesmen were? they were Major W. Sudell and N. L. Jackson the father of the Corinthians, North End played the Corinthians game with this difference, they were slightly too clever and elaborated too much, and therefore lost time on the way, the Corinthians being quicker in getting from one end to the other, that is as far as my experience goes. At the same time North End were the finest side who ever stepped onto a football field and were got together by Major Sudell within 2 years of the adoption of professionalism. We played North End in a charity match in London in 1886 - 1887, at the same time that the London - Scottish were playing a rugby game with Blackheath, and that was the very first game ever graced by royalty, The Prince of Wales, later of course king Edward VII, attended accompanied by his son, The Duke of Clarence, I have always had a great fondness for professionals and I always found them to be just as much gentlemen as any other players. Years ago I expressed my views with regard to the maximum wage clause, I held them then and I hold them now, that if a man is worth £3 a week he should be paid that sum, whilst if he is worth £40 a week he should still receive the sum, to say that he shall not be paid what he is worth is absurd. Before leaving all reference to the Corinthians I may point out that in their December winter tour in 1884 they played 6 games in one week. As 20 players on tour they beat Blackburn Rovers on the Monday 8 - 1 lost to Darwen on Tuesday 2 - 1, drew with Blackburn Olympic on Wednesday 4 - 4, beat Sheffield and lost to Preston North End 3 - 1, then the following Monday lost to Notts County 3 - 2. Our defence was rather weak, for we were without the brothers A. M. and P. M. Walters, but amongst those that did assist us was J. A. Dixon of Notts County and afterwards captain of Notts County Cricket eleven. Two of the best inside forwards I ever played with were Fred Dewhurst and John Goodall both of Preston North End, both seemed to know exactly what there fellow players were going to do before it happened, their intuition was really amazing and they actually made openings for the player who was running with the ball, it is often said that the man with the ball should make the opening but it is just as much the duty of the other forwards to get into positions so that they can play up to him.

THE FINER POINTS

Along with these two I would bracket the brothers W. F. and R. C. Gosling of the Corinthians, and I must record what two powerful backs P. M. and A. M. Walters were, David Russell of Preston and Nottm Forest was the best half-back I have played against, he seemed to know what one was going to do, and it was difficult to deceive him. He was quick and had a wonderful knowledge of the finer points of the game. Other players I would like to refer to are Dennis Hodgetts of Aston Villa and Billy Bassett of West Bromich, in a cup semi-final at Derby, during a snowstorm Bassett was so elusive, that it was said he hid behind the snowflakes. The story is rivalled by one concerning a game between Nottingham Forest and Preston, the encounter took place on the old town ground at Nottingham, which was noted for a profuse growth of crocuses every spring, the Forest won and North End explained their defeat by saying that they could not see the ball for crocuses.

ENGLISH RECORD

Tinsley Lindley played in 13 internationals, 5 against Scotland, 4 against Wales, 4 against Ireland and was captain when England beat Scotland 5-0 at Glasgow in 1888 scoring 3 goals, that being the biggest victory ever gained by England in these encounters, and the first in the last 10 played, I would not like to say that it was the best team which represented England, but Dennis Hodgetts write-up afterwards said it had the best forward line. Perhaps the side who accomplished such a splendid performance will be of interest, it was as follows:- W. R. Moon, P. M. Walters, J. Holden White, R. Haworth, G. Haworth, J. Woodhall, G. Goodhall, T. Lindley, F. Dewhurst, A. Allen.

I was always ready to accept an invite to play and the following list will give an idea of the part of the games I played for:- Corinthians, Cambridge & Oxford, North & South Nottinghamshire & Sheffield, London & Middlesex, Preston North End, The Swifts, England Casuals & Gentlemen's Club and both Notts Clubs.

At rugby football I played for Cambridge, Notts and The Old Leysians. My jerseys you will agree were of many colours. In all my games I took greatest delight in my appearance for Notts County. It proved costly to the club, their usual centre forward, James Oswald was under suspension and being in difficulty about filling his place, the committee asked me to take it, the game was against Aston Villa and we succeeded in making a draw.

RUBBING IT IN

The Villa were annoyed and lodged an appeal with the league, and Notts were fined £5 and ordered to have one point deducted, Notts were dissatisfied with the decision and lodged another appeal and there was some consternation amongst their officials when their fine was increased to £30 and 2 points deducted from their record, I also played once for Preston North End’s 1st professional team and may I say that I was always fond of them, it is impossible to say how many goals I scored, but I know I played in matches in which plenty were obtained without kicking one myself.

MODERN FAULTS

In one Oxford and Cambridge match, when captain, I went straight from kick-off and scored without an Oxford player touching the ball and I repeated that performance in a game at Preston, I consider that this should be done more often than it is, ball control nowadays is bad and shooting is a faulty as it can be.

Forwards will not get their knees over the ball, they shoot off the toe-cap instead of the instep. Players on the wings should be taught the principles of the tangents and angles with a moving ball, they should have their feet at a certain angle, receive it, and they would see it go back to the player who is dashing through. From my point of view, the changes that have been made in the game have brought about deteriation, the result of playing what is called the W. Formation, is that at least one of two players are often off-side, the forwards should help each other and go ahead together.

2 REFEREES

Another reason for the decline is that for some reason or another, the backs and half-backs play the wrong game. In my opinion it is the duty of the half-back to watch the outside man, the reverse action is often seen and it is a mistaken policy. In a lecture I gave to the Nottingham Forest club in 1905, I dealt with referees, because they do their work in the spirit of the game, no amount of theory can create that splendid breath for football that comes from actual practice. Another point upon which I feel strongly about is that referees should base their decisions on the intention of the act and not on the mere consequence of it, no penalty line,. Then again I consider that there should be two referees, one for each half of the field, I also hold that the penalty line should be abolished, for the players should not be allowed to know where they can or cannot trip with impunity. I do not consider it right that a player should be able to say to himself, "inside that line I must not be unfair, outside of it I can be so if I like". I would therefore do away with the lines and give powers to the referees to award penalty kicks for foul play over a much larger area than at present.

WENT TO SLEEP

While playing association football, I also played rugby, I got my college colours and afterwards played for Notts and the Old Leysians, I also played cricket and narrowly missed out getting my blue, against the Australians.

In 1893 I appeared in the Oxford and Cambridge team, the tourists kept us in the field all Thursday and Friday and part of Saturday, scoring 843 runs, I remember that afterwards I had to be woke up to go into bat, we scored 191 and 82 for one wicket and so the match ended in a draw. My first cricket match for Notts was against Surrey in 1888 and I scored 40 and 7, I also played for Notts against the Australians and I have recollections of a great catch I made which got rid of Worrall, William Gunn had been placed in the spot where it was supposed Worrall would hit the ball, but instead of doing this, the batsman sent it sky high in my direction, I was in a terrible state, but I put out my hands and the ball just dropped into them and stuck.

SERVICE FOR FOOTBALL PLAYERS

The demon of misgiving has me in his grip and the experience is extremely disconcerting. I like not the way Forest have played in these last 2 matches and more especially am I worried about the harsh things which it was necessary to say of Saturdays encounter at White Hart Lane. We will admit that the ground conditions were bad, the surface had a sort of plasticine texture that was taxing on the physical stamina more than ordinary mud, but the playing piece was the same for both sides, it was no softer at one end than the other and the Spurs ploughed through it as though there was nothing wrong whatsoever. Speaking of Tottenham's performance it was masterly, except when the forwards approached the goal, Forest on the other hand, erred in various directions, and no where more obviously than at wing half. The visiting forwards were not good come to that, but if How and Buckingham who were outstanding had been playing in their rear, we should have seen a difference, it was those two gentlemen occupying the corresponding positions to Edgar and Pugh who did more than anybody to win the match for their side.

IS TRAINING OVER DONE

As luck would have it, Dr. Tinsley Lindley had selected Saturday as an occasion for one of his few outing's with the old club of which for many years ago he was a famous player, I did not ask him what he thought of the result, but I was richer in knowledge for a very interesting talk with the great "Corinthian" centre forward, on the way back from St. Pancras to Nottingham. In the first place I was made to realise how the years are speeding by, when Dr. Lindley told me that in his day, so far as he could remember, there was no professional side in the south of England, no West Ham, Charlton, Brentford, Millwall, Tottenham, Arsenal or Chelsea. We discussed the question of training and the elaborate preparations which the modern day player undergoes for an hour and a half exertion on a Saturday afternoon. Dr. Lindley did not believe the players were much better for all this special training, he thought it over-done, and added, "I think a lot more could be learned if players were to attend a school of geometry and study what I call the reflex of the ball, the angle it makes, they would appreciate then that there is no reason why a player should not shoot from any angle so long as he gets his knee over the ball".

IN DR. LINDLEYS DAYS

I ventured to point out that there was a general feeling that the present day game was a good deal faster than the play of the old day, again Dr. Lindley was not in agreement, on the contrary he continued that football was as fast in 1889-1890, because in those times the whole of the forwards were going down the line with the ball, which was always kept ahead of the man never being more than 2 feet off the ground, “In my time” he continued, “I do not think there was a Corinthian who could not do a 100 yards in his togs in just over 11 seconds. Full-backs were, I am sure, faster than they are now". At White Hart Lane last Saturday was the scene of a very interesting reunion, Mr. W. Moon, who is a well known solicitor came along to renew acquaintance with Dr. Lindley who was leading the Forest line when in the 1880s Forest met Notts and Mr. Moon was keeping goal for Notts.

LIFE MEMBERS OF THE FOREST CLUB

Two names were added to the list, Mr. F. Forman and Dr. Tinsley Lindley. The Forest life membership is not an extensive one and there are 4 surviving names at present on the list:- J. Rawson, R. G. Hogarth, H. Heath and H. R. Rawson.

Tinsley Lindley now a prominent barrister won 13 caps for England as a centre forward, he also played many times for Nottingham Forest as well as for the Corinthians, (of which he is also a life member), the London Swifts and Crusaders. One noted writer at the time when Dr. Lindley was in his prime described him as an ideal centre forward in an ideal international team, Besides Forest, he also figured in Notts County ranks and once turned out for Oxford University, although he was at Cambridge, Dr. Lindley also played cricket for Notts on several occasions, one of them being against the Australians at Trent Bridge, the tourists being defeated on that occasion. He was also prominent at the rugby game, as a member of the Old Leysians and the Notts Rugby Clubs Boxing, Swimming are other sports that have claimed and still claim Dr. Lindleys interest.

Mr. Frank Forman, who has been on the clubs management for many years, played his first game in the red garabaldi, in 1895 and as right and centre half, was deservedly awarded international honours in 1898, 1899, 1901 and 1902 for Scotland, 1899 and 1903 for Wales 1898, 1899 and 1902 for Ireland.

WHEN TINSLEY LINDLEY DID THE HAT-TRICK

Not since February 5th, 1887, the year of Queen Victoria's jubilee, have England and Ireland met at Bramall Lane, so their meeting at the Sheffield United HQ on Monday will be a worthy event. That long ago international was won by England by 7 goals to 0 and we are reminded that in that remarkable encounter one of the scorers was Tinsley Lindley of the Forest and the Corinthians who did the hat-trick. Association football in Ireland in those long ago days was in it's infancy and victory for the saxons was a foregone conclusion, there was some superb goalkeeping by Gillespie of Hertford who was described as the prince of goalkeepers.

W. N. Cobbold and Fred Dewhurst equally shared the other 4 goals and the England team was:- H. Arthur (Blackburn), G. Howarth (P.N.E.), E. Mason (Wolves), H. Forrest (Blackburn), E. Brayshaw (Sheff. Wed.), G. Howarth (Accrington), J. Sayer (Stoke), F. Dewhurst (P.N.E.), T. Lindley (Forest & Corinthians), E. Bambridge (Swifts) and W. N. Cobbold (Carthusians). Umpire, Mr. J. C. Clegg (now a Sir).

Old followers of the game will recall the abilities of those players. Cobbold is always spoken of as "The Prince of Dribblers". The international matches of the present day remind you that it is a long time since a Nottingham born player appeared in the England v Scotland fixture and a considerable time since a local amateur gained a Scotch cap. There was a time when Nottingham amateurs were to the fore in association football, the old days of Billy Gunn are but memories, just as the name of Stuart McCrae is but a name to many.

A NOTTS STALWART

In the international match in which McCrae appeared, it was said that N. C. Bailey, the famous English half-back, was not on par excellence on the English side, McCrae being in the ascendancy and indeed the Notts amateur played better than any of the halves on either the English or Scotch side, Johnny Kaye found in him his match and he played for the Corinthians against the then famous Queens Park at the Oval in 1885, and on other occasions, in the sensational match against Bolton Wanderers, McCrae enabled Notts to score, amid the wildest excitement, the famous struggle is spoken of even today in Bolton by old followers of soccer and how Notts won after a most desperate struggle, it was one of McCrae's happiest memories, he played in 5 international games and it would have been a difficult task to have found a better all round athlete in his day.

FAMOUS LOCAL AMATEURS

The fact is that in the old days no international team was complete without an amateur and conversely today the difficulty is to find one good enough, proves something that England versus Scotland eleven even in the prime of professional days had as their first choice for goal an amateur in the person of W. R. Moon which is a feather in the cap of amateurism, P. M. Walters was one of the backs and in the forward line was our own Tinsley Lindley leading the van, Chadwick and Denny Hodgetts on the left flank, Hodgetts was a fine player, always full of enthusiasm, to illustrate this a story was told to this effect that the Villa arrived late on the ground in one away game leaving barely 5 minutes to strip and appear on the field, there was a censure and a fine against a team for not being on time and Denny was captain that day. He entreated his comrades to hurry up and proceed to set an example, "come on lads", he called to them as he prepared to leave the dressing room. He started out to lead his men on the field, but a loud shout of unseemly mirth called to his attention to the fact that although he had on his boots and pads, there was still an important part of the regulation attire lacking and Denny had to beat a retreat to put them on, but again I digress, Denny was a great strategist and a magnificent forward and football was football in those days.

There were 4 amateurs in the English team against Scotland in 1893, Gay in goal, Harrison at back and Gosling captained the side against the Scots in 1895. When another amateur in Lodge was at back, Reynolds, Holt and Needham, were the other halves that day, can you imagine a trio of greater worriers.?

I must recall the forward line too, because it was colloquially speaking, “hot stuff", A right wing like Bassett, and Bloomer could not be beaten, especially with Johnny Goodall in the centre, Gosling and Smith of the Villa, were on the left. Mention of Bloomer calls to mind that I was present at the first international trial match in 1895 which Steve Bloomer played along side Bassett, the fixture took place on the Trent Bridge ground, the two busy bees swamped the opposing defence, I was standing on the touchline with a colleague against where Bassett was operating, as goal after goal was scored, some from his wonderful centres, he turned to us and asked how many is that? I think the answer was 9. Bloomer showed great promise that day, Lindley playing alongside Johnny Goodall who was one of the greatest amateur forwards of his day and since, and England was merry Old England then winning 5 - 0.

The next season marked the last appearance of the Walters and the following season for Lindley who left his interest in the crossbar to be called to the other bar. The famous Forester played against the Thistle on 5 consecutive occasions from 1886 to 1890. The next season found Moon retaining his place in goal, with a pair of professional backs Holmes and Howarth in front of him. Our special interest in the side was Albert Smith the Forest amateur half-back one of the finest intermediates in the country, a player who knew how to break up an advance and initiate an attack on his wing. In the centre of the middle line was little Johnny Holt and another local favourite in Alf Shelton, there never was a greater man at heading the ball than him. It was Alf’s cranium before everybodies and they used to say that he would have been a great footballer even if he never used his feet at all.

NOTTINGHAM INTERNATIONALS

Fred Geary, another Nottingham born lad was in the same international side. He was one of the nippiest centre forwards that ever flashed through a defence, he was an Everton player and he was a fine shot at goal. I shall never forget playing alongside him once, not in a international match, let me add, but in a scratch match on the Forest recreation ground in the early days of my youth. In the international match referred to the whole of the front line of England were pros, imagine a lineup like this, Billy Bassett and Johnny Goodhall on the right, Geary in the centre and his club mates Chadwick and Millward on the left. When George Toone, the Notts goalie was in goal for England that was a fine year, George was a character in his way and his fump as he called thumping the ball, was only equalled in his own enjoyment when he could tipple an opposing forward over on his back, those were the merry old days when a goalkeepers lot was not a happy one.

Before protection for goalkeepers, for the backs he had in front of him A. T. B. Dunn the famous amateur, with Bob Holmes as partner and the halves consisted of daddy Reynolds, Johnny Holt and Toones club mate Alf Shelton, once again, I am digressing from my theme (I often do) but cannot help mentioning the forward line, there were Billy Bassett and Johnny Goodhall again on the right, Southwarth one of the brainiest centres, it was the beginning of the derby mans rise to fame, there are many times when we sit in front of the fire in our carpet slippers and think of the glorious dash of Bloomers against Scotland, a rush which nonplussed the Scottish backs and won the game for England.

THE REAL OLD DAYS

But of course your quite right, we set out to talk about old Nottingham players especially amateurs. My digressions are getting a bit of a habit here. Again I am to use another colloquialism up against it, for in conversation with an old follower of football whose talk of the best days make my old days seem quite young days, I am told that the best days were those when, Sammy Widdowson led the Forest team, when Teddy Leighton made his electric runs down the wing and when Tommy Hancock scattered the opposing forwards right and left and when Danks and Norman were the names to conjure with. Also for the old reds, in the Notts camp there were E. H, Greenhalgh, who played back for England and in the first match against Scotland, Harry Moore a stalwart defender, Arthur Cursham and the great Morecai Sherwin who filled the goal, William Gunn, before mentioned and Johnny Dixon were forwards of great note in their day and Harry Jackson is a name that will come to mind. Both J. A. Dixon and H. Jackson played in local amateur football when in the veteran stage and I remember as a young beginner playing against the latter just before he put up his football boots for the last time, I always tried to remember one or two things that he told me, Dobson, Harker and Emmett were other names.

PAST AND PRESENT

My own personal recollections are more of the period, when Harry Daft flashed along the left wing for the county, and when Frank Forman showed us what half-back play really was, and later when Walter Ball led the magpies, but all the old stagers of every generation will tell you that football today is not anything like so good as it used to be, it never was.

THE ENGLAND ELEVEN OF 1890

Howarth, Holmes, Shelton *(Notts)*, A. Smith *(Forest)*, Bassett, Goodhall, Geary *(Notts)*, Chadwick, Millward, W. R. Moon, Holt when 3 Notts men were in the team.

THE CORINTHIANS TEAM THAT PRACTICALLY MADE THE ENGLAND TEAM

N. L. Jackson, J. L. Nickisson, M. J. Rendall, J. Holm, B. W. Spilsbury, Dr. J. N. O. Smith, A. Amos, C. W. R. Tepper, W. N. Cobbold, T. Lindley, F. W. Pawson, C. Holden White, A. Watson and T. Pellatt.

Corinthians played their first match on November 1st 1882, among the outstanding players who have been associated with the club are many who are household words, in the annals of English sport, including G. O. Smith and C. B. Fry, but Nottingham football owes much to the Corinthians because they gave to it Tinsley Lindley. Skillful play and enthusiastic personality helped to build up the great traditions of the game that are the heritage of all who represent our two premier clubs. Another Nottingham man who played for the Corinthians is mayor J. D, Barnsdale, a former officer of the Robin Hoods and brother-in-law of the well known firm of silk merchants of Warser Gate, Nottingham.

Dr. Lindley is a ruddier of countenance than it used to be, at certain moments he bears a strange resemblance to the Mr. E. V. Lucus and has kind of a connection with Punch, for he married a daughter of the late Sir Francis Burnard, Phil May was one of his closest friends and often visited him when in Nottinghamshire.

SANDY HIGGINS

T. Lindley played for Nottingham Forest as well as the Corinthians. When Forest turned professional a Scottish centre forward came along, a talented player and a great character named Sandy Higgins. T. Lindley then took one of the inside positions. The last I heard of Sandy Higgins said Dr. Lindley, was when he came from Scotland to join in some celebrations, I was not in Nottingham that day, but Sandy was bent on seeing me, it proved to be a merry affair, and late at night Sandy was in Nottingham market place asking a policeman for my address.

THERE WAS ONLY 3 LEFT IN 1938

In 1885 Nottingham Forest having drawn 1 - 1 at Derby 10 days later they replayed their F.A. Cup Semi-Final with Queens Park at Edinburgh, and lost 3 -1. Today their are only 3 men alive out of the 22 who took to the field on that occasion, Dr. Lindley, J. E. Leighton F. W. Beardsley, the last surviving member of the opposition died last year, their centre forward, D. Smith, age

82 years Mr. Leighton, who still lives and carries on business in Nottingham, bears his age well, and though it was as far back as 1889 when he finished his active career with the Forest and the famous Corinthians, the International who appeared at outside left for England against Ireland at Belfast in 1886 is still one of soccer's most enthusiastic followers.

WHERE ARE THEY NOW

Forest are not what they were, I am afraid was his remark to the Free Foresters, but then how many of the old clubs are as good, the game has altered very considerably since the 90's when ariel passing was a crime and there were hosts of deadly marksmen who could shoot with either foot, where are the shots at the present time who can equal Steve Bloomer, Jimmy Ross of Preston North End and W. N. Cobbold of the Corinthians and Cambridge University, who was capped 5 times against Scotland, 4 times Ireland and 4 against Wales, there are few now to equal those giants, although I should include Gallagar of Notts County as one of the nearest approaches, he is a great player, I will say however, that football as I see it now seems to be gradually coming back to the old style.

Mr. Leighton recalled that he was one of several players including A. W Ward, W. Hancock and F. Fox, the late Nottingham Forest treasurer, who graduated to the Forest club from Nottingham Swifts, as his memory searched back through the years he lived again some of the historic cup matches in which he was engaged, I remember he said that I came into the Forest team for the cup engagement with Queens Park, because the week previous G. Unwin at outside left had broken his collar bone against Blackburn Rovers on the Old Parkside Ground, it was perhaps a dubious consolation, that Unwin sustained his injury in a tussle with Ferguson Suter, the Rovers right back, who was the first professional ever to come to England.

In the preceeding round Queens Park whom we first played at Derby, and replayed at Edinburgh had defeated Notts County at the Trent Bridge Ground by the only goal scored and that came from Arnott at full-back, who completely surprised Dr. Coulby the County keeper, the score was 1 - 1 at Derby, but in Scotland we went down by 3 goals to 0.

John Edward Leighton, Nottingham Forest - Corinthians - England

He was one of the last three players of the 22 left alive in 1938 from the game between Nottingham Forest and Queens Park played at Edinburgh in the replay of the English Cup which Forest lost by 3 goals to 1. The last member of the opposition died last year 1937, their centre forward D. Smith, aged 82 years.

Athletic News
And Competitors' Guide.

PLAYERS Worth £40WE

FAMOUS CORINTHIAN INTERNATIONAL'S FOOTBALL REFORMS.

DR. TINSLEY LINDLEY.

ENGLISH CUP SEMI-FINAL

GARIBALDI COLOURS. **IN SCOTLAND.** TWO FAMOUS BROTHERS.

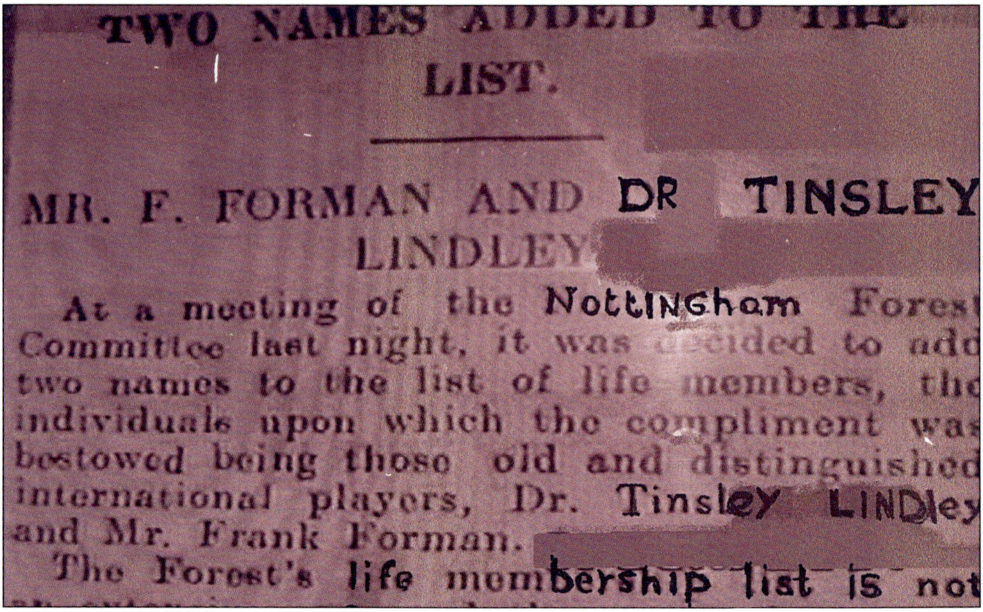

TWO NAMES ADDED TO THE LIST.

MR. F. FORMAN AND DR TINSLEY LINDLEY

At a meeting of the Nottingham Forest Committee last night, it was decided to add two names to the list of life members, the individuals upon which the compliment was bestowed being those old and distinguished international players, Dr. Tinsley LINDley and Mr. Frank Forman.

The Forest's life membership list is not

NO PENALTY LINE

Then again, I consider that ther
hould be two referees—one for eac
alf of the field.

I also hold that the penalty lin
hould be abolished, for players shoul
ot be allowed to know where the
an or cannot trip with impunity.

I do not consider it right that
player should be able to say to him
self: "Inside that line I SHALL NOT b
unfair; outside it I can be so if I like.

A friend bet him a case of champagne that he did not do the hat-trick, but Lindley got five in the last ten minutes! A total of 85 goals in one season for Forest. The Dr. says latter day forwards are afraid to shoot and don't know how to!

for some reason or other, the backs and half-backs play the wrong game. In my opinion it is the job of the half-back to watch the outside forward and for the back to take the *inside* man. The reverse action is often seen, and it is a mistaken policy.

In a lecture I gave to the Nottingham Forest club in 1905 I dealt with referees, past, present, and future. Old players, in my opinion, make the best referees, because they do their work in the spirit of the game. No

TINSLEY LINDLEY. NOTTS FOREST

Lindley for the Reds. In 1882 he scored 85 goals off his own boot—as many as some teams score in a season at the present day!

Three years later he put the ball into the net 59 times in 46 matches!

What a centre-forward, and how the opposition quailed!

TINSLEY LINDLEY is a doctor of laws. He still takes an interest in Nottingham athletics, but thinks that some of the young runners of to-day are not keen on training.

"I saw a young fellow come to run the 100 yards the other day," he told me. "As he came to the track he threw away a cigarette."

RUBBING IT IN

The Villa were very annoyed and lodged an appeal with the League, and Notts were fined £5 and ordered to have one point deducted. Notts were dissatisfied with the decision and lodged another appeal, and there was some consternation amongst their officials when their fine was increased to £30 and two points were deducted from their record!

I also played once for Preston North End's first professional team, and I may say that I was always very fond

I became captain of the school team, and when I was little over 16 years of age I joined Nottingham Forest, playing with some regularity for them for two years. In my first game for the Forest against Wolverhampton at Stafford-road I scored three goals.

Going up to Cambridge I secured my colours in my first year, and I was captain for two years—in 1886-1887. Being elected a member of the Corinthians I remander a playing member of that organisation until I retired from football in 1895 or 1896.

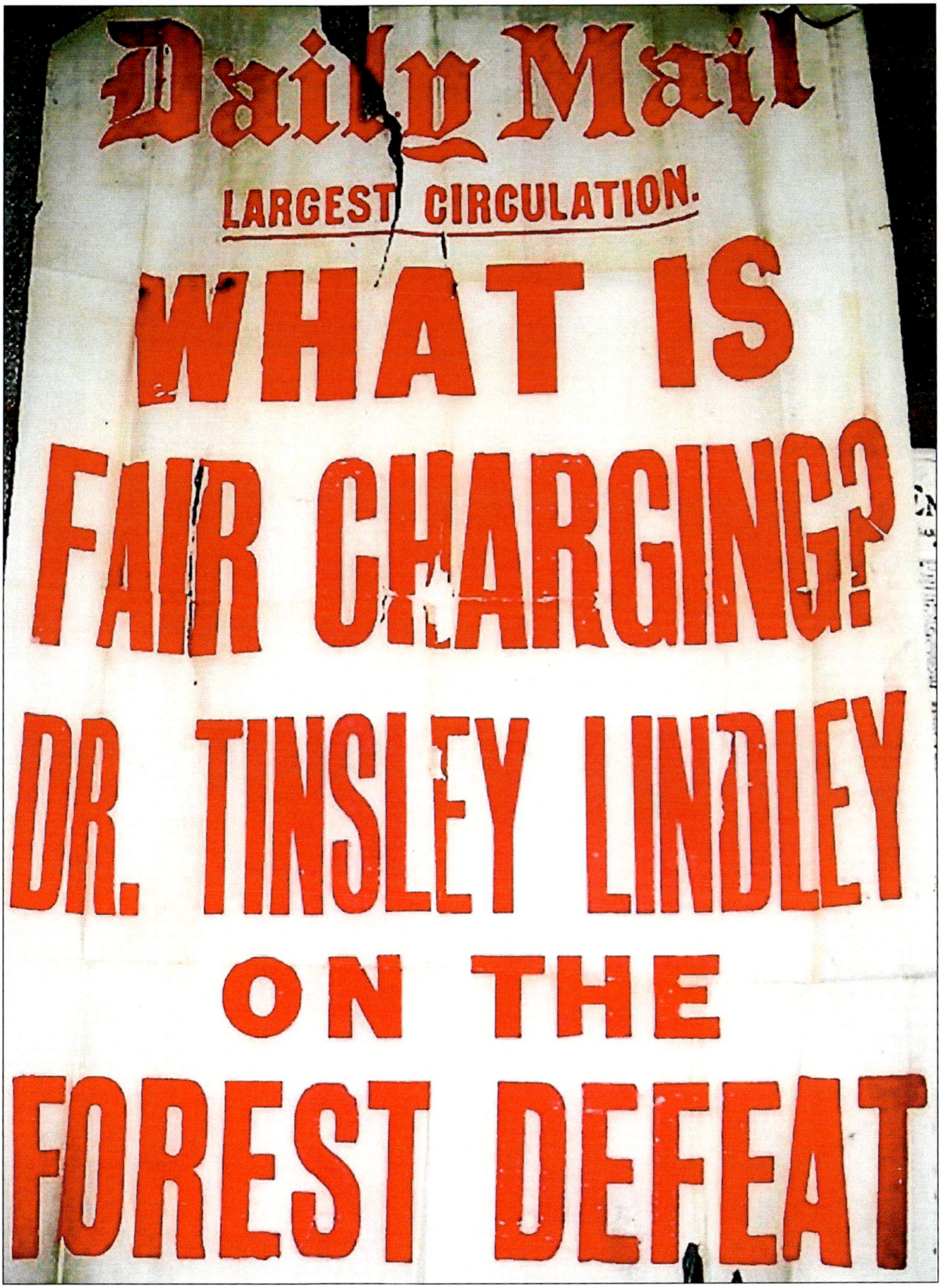

A Daily Mail newspaper billboard when Tinsley Lindley was a sports correspondent

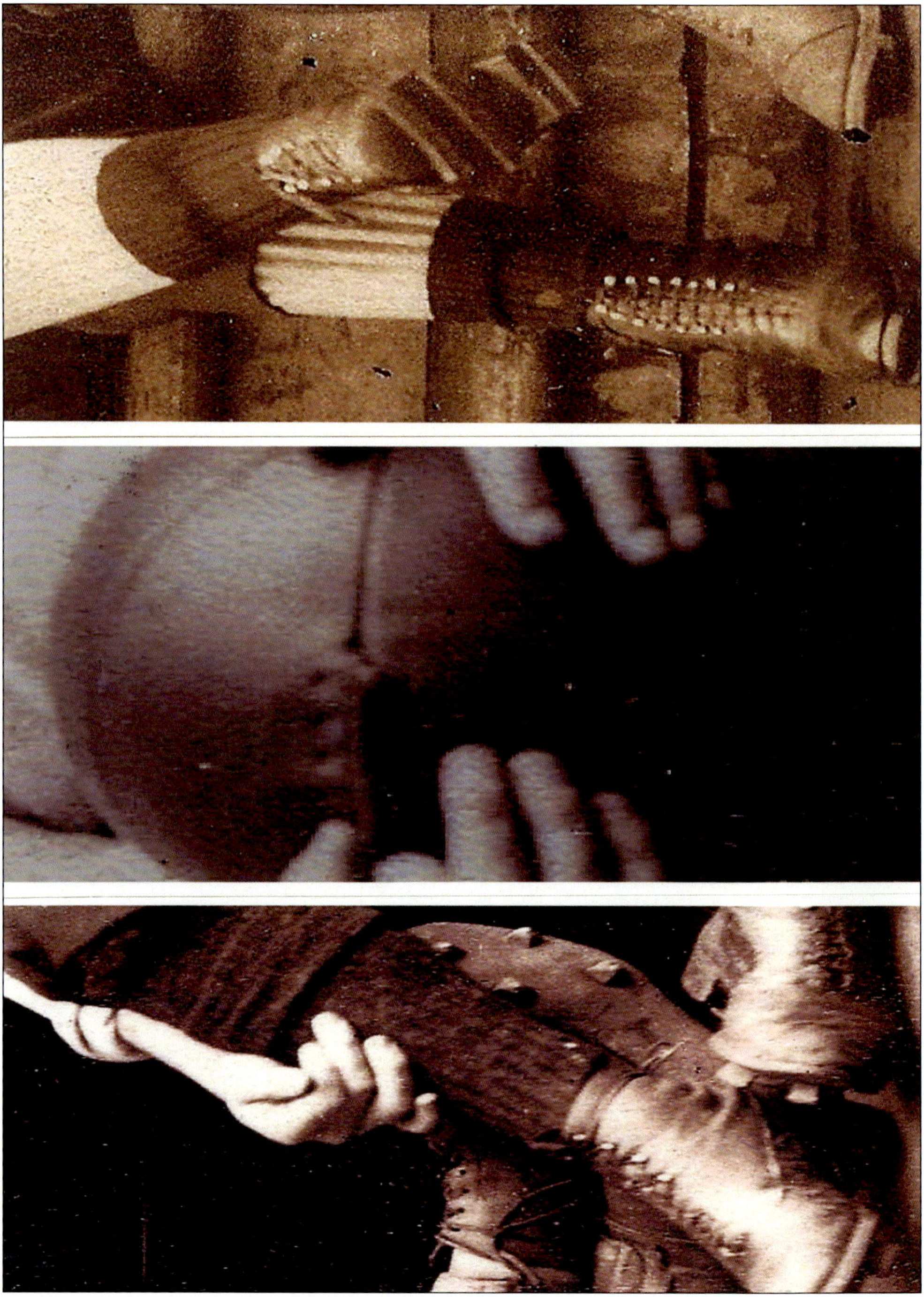

Footballers ball boots and pads worn in the 1880s

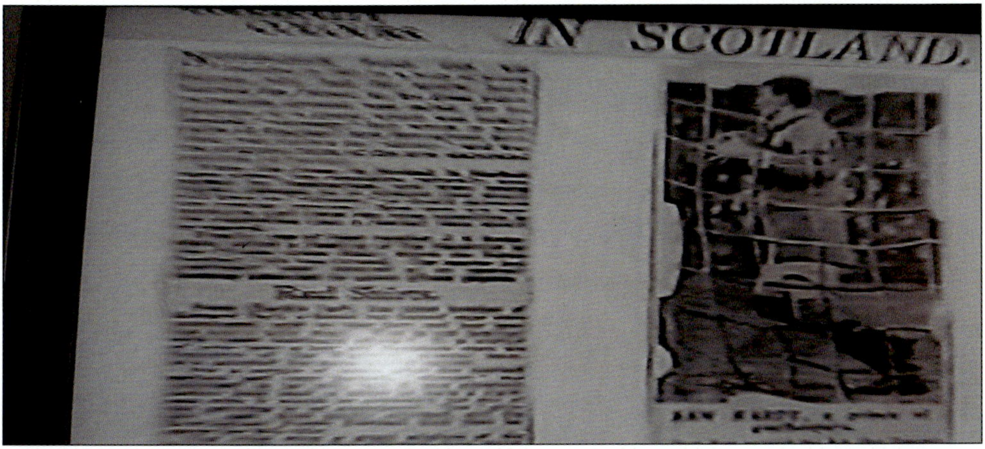

IN SCOTLAND.

"Watchman" Tells How Nottingham Forest Lost An

ENGLISH CUP SEMI-FINAL

GARIBALDI COLOURS.

IN SCOTLAND.

TWO FAMOUS BROTHERS.

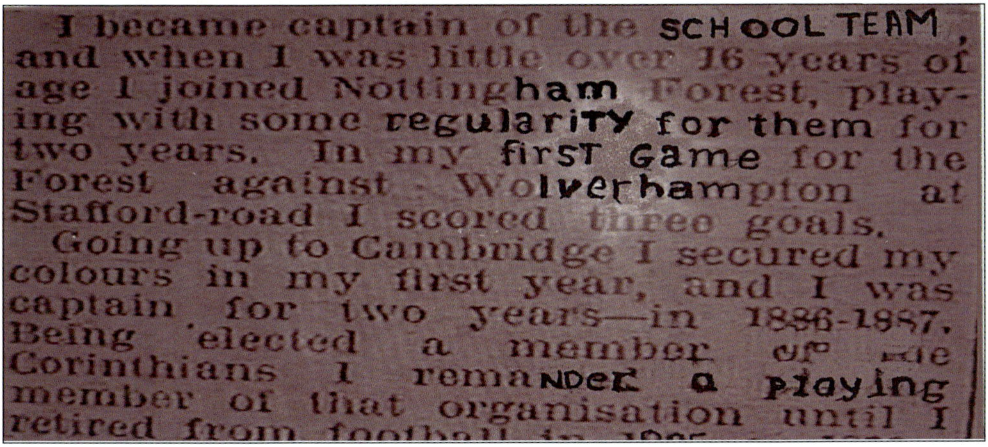

I became captain of the SCHOOL TEAM, and when I was little over 16 years of age I joined Nottingham Forest, playing with some regularity for them for two years. In my first Game for the Forest against Wolverhampton at Stafford-road I scored three goals.

Going up to Cambridge I secured my colours in my first year, and I was captain for two years—in 1886-1887. Being elected a member of the Corinthians I remander a playing member of that organisation until I retired from football in

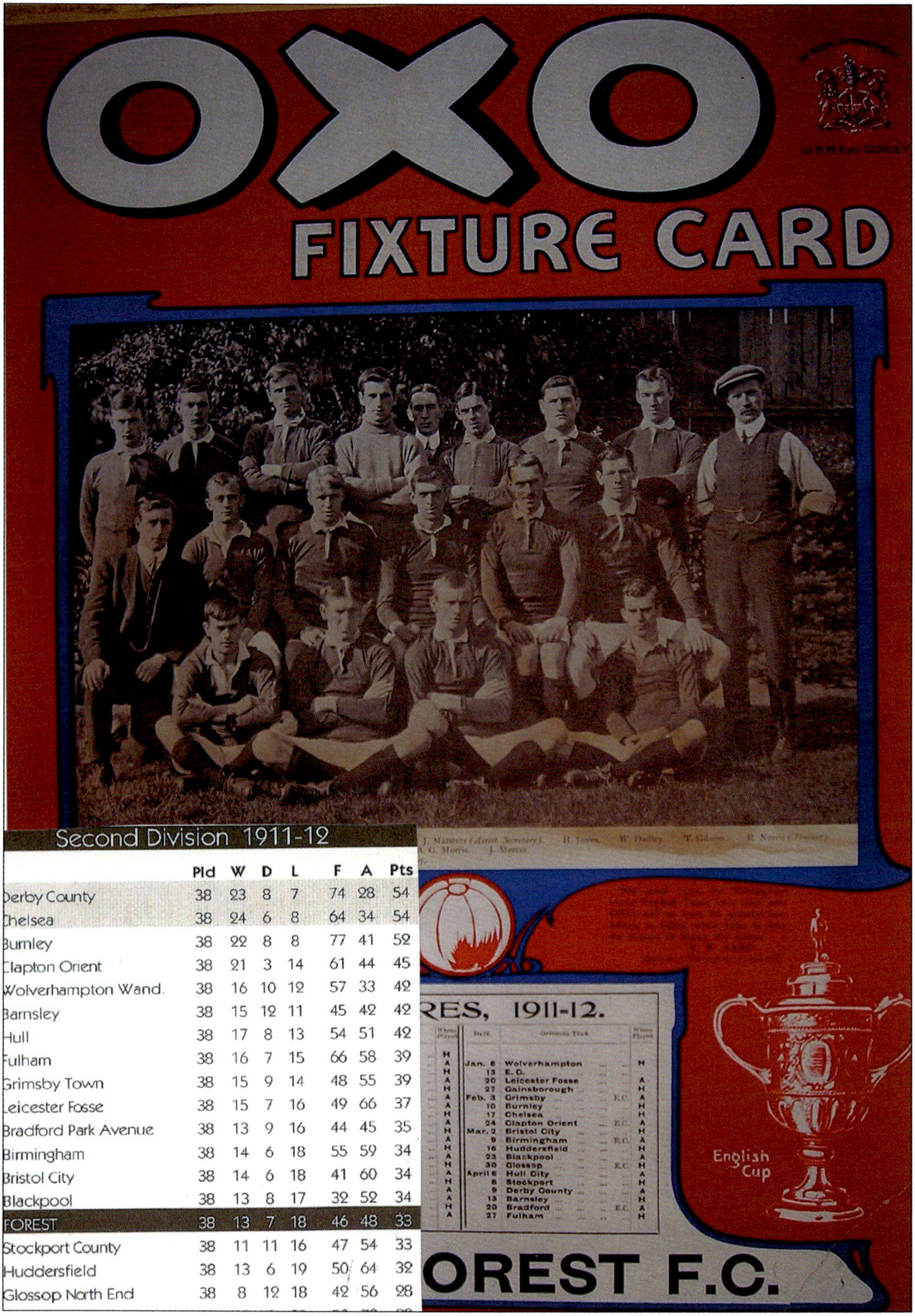

Second Division 1911-12

	Pld	W	D	L	F	A	Pts
Derby County	38	23	8	7	74	28	54
Chelsea	38	24	6	8	64	34	54
Burnley	38	22	8	8	77	41	52
Clapton Orient	38	21	3	14	61	44	45
Wolverhampton Wand.	38	16	10	12	57	33	42
Barnsley	38	15	12	11	45	42	42
Hull	38	17	8	13	54	51	42
Fulham	38	16	7	15	66	58	39
Grimsby Town	38	15	9	14	48	55	39
Leicester Fosse	38	15	7	16	49	66	37
Bradford Park Avenue	38	13	9	16	44	45	35
Birmingham	38	14	6	18	55	59	34
Bristol City	38	14	6	18	41	60	34
Blackpool	38	13	8	17	32	52	34
FOREST	38	13	7	18	46	48	33
Stockport County	38	11	11	16	47	54	33
Huddersfield	38	13	6	19	50	64	32
Glossop North End	38	8	12	18	42	56	28

A. G. Morris

Aberystwyth - Swindon Town - Nottingham Forest

scored 217 goals for Nottingham Forest, played for Wales between 1906-1911, gaining 21 caps.

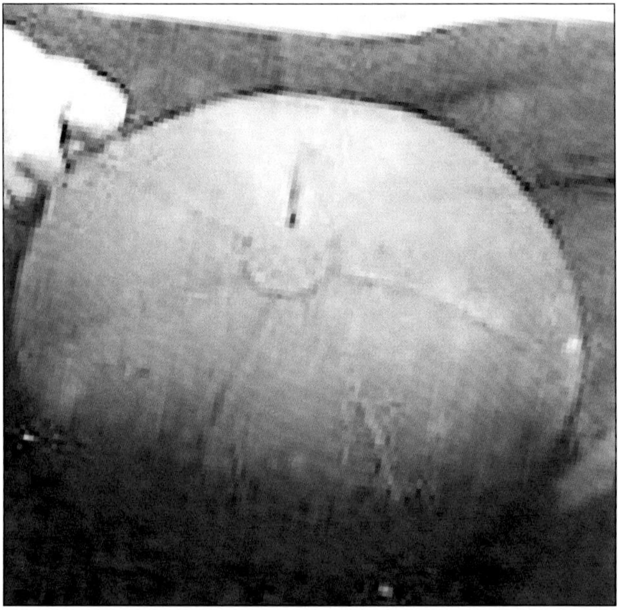

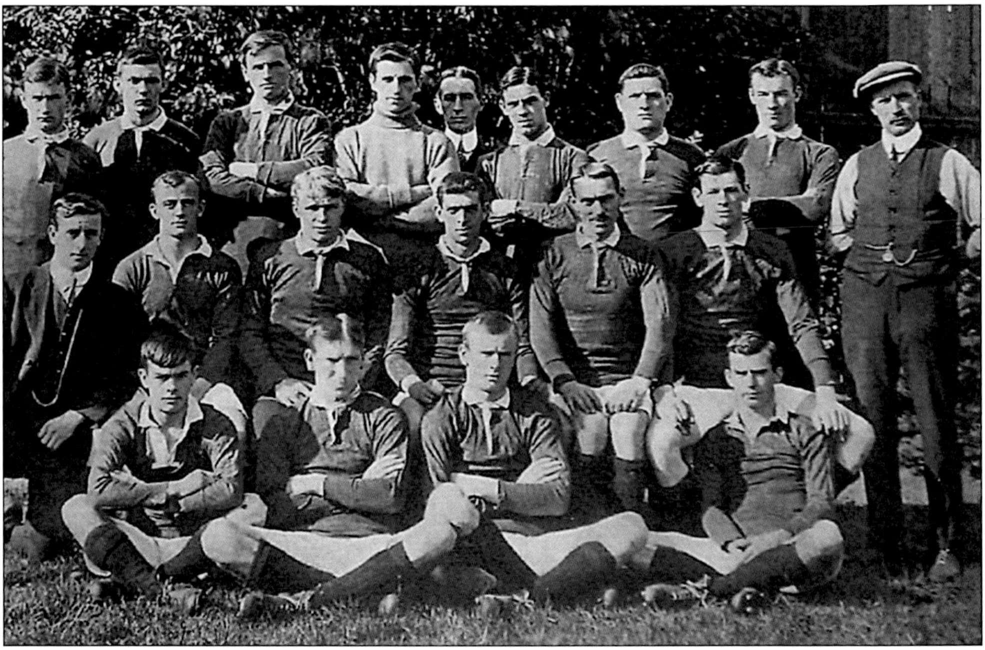

Nottingham Forest 1911-1912
Back Row: J. Ford, F, Langham, J. Hanna, R. Masters, H, Jones, W. Dudley, T. Gibson, R. Norris (Trainer)
Middle Row: F. Banks, W, Hooper, A. Fisher, J. Armstrong, A. G. Morris, J. Mercer
Front Row: J. Derrick, F. Saunders, G. Needham, G. Maltby

NOTTS FOREST TEAM 1884-1885. SEASON.
T. DANKS-C. CABORN-S. WIDDOWSON-T. LINDLEY
H. BILLYEALD-T. HANCOCK-F. FOX-A. WARD

NOTTINGHAM FOREST FOOTBALL TEAM. 1887-1888, SEASON.
BACK ROW. LEFT TO RIGHT,- HARRY PIKE,- FRED FOX,- GEORGE TUTIN,- WILLIAM HANCOCK,- TINSLEY LINDLEY,- CLUB REF. UNKNOWN.
MIDDLE ROW LEFT TO RIGHT,- FRANK BURTON,- SALATHIEL NORMAN,- CHARLES CABORN,- THOMAS DANKS.
FRONT ROW, LEFT TO RIGHT,- HENRY BILLYEALD,- ARTHUR PIKE, JOHN EDWARD LEIGHTON.

SOME OF NOTTM FOREST MATCHES
1886 UNTILL 1898

DAY	MTH.	YEAR	OPP.	GRD.	SCORE	SCORERS
		1866	NOTTS C.	FOREST REC	1--0	W.H.REVIS
16th.	NOV.	1878	NOTTS C.	BEESTON	3--1	?
8th.	NOV.	1879	NOTTS C.	TRENT BR.	4--0	?
17th.	JAN.	1880	NOTTS C.	TRENT BR.	7--1	?
16th.	DEC.	1880	NOTTS C.	TRENT BR.	4--0	?
6th.	MARCH	1881	NOTTS C.	CASTLE GR.	1--0	?
17th.	DEC.	1881	NOTTS C.	TRENT BR.	5--0	?
14th.	OCT.	1882	B/BURN.OLYP.	TRENT BR.	1--0	(HARP INJURED)
17th.	FEB.	1882	WOLVES	STAFFORD Rd	6--1.	danks 1, widdowson 1. billyeald.1, lindley 3.
24th.	FEB.	1882	WOLVES	TRENT BR.	6--0.	danks 1, billyeald 1. widdowson 1. l
	MARCH	1882				?
10th.	MARCH.	1882	WED.OLD ATH.	CASTLE .GR.	5--1.	fletcher 2.lindley billyeald
17th.	MARCH	1882	WED.OLD ATH.	CASTLE GR.	3--1.	danks 2. lindley 1
19th.	MAY	1883	WEST BROM.	PERRY BARR	5--3.	
20th.	JAN.	1883	NOTTS C.	TRENT BR.	1--1	
26th.	MARCH	1883	STOKE	STOKE.	11--2.	
20th.	OCT.	1883	NOTTS C.	PARKSIDE	0--0	
27th.	NOV.	1883	DUMBARTON	PARKSIDE	2--3	widdowson 2.
7th.	MARCH	1885	BLACKBURN	PARKSIDE	3--0	

(G.UNWIN BREAKS COLLAR BONE IN A TUSSLE WITH FURGUSON SUTER THE FIRST PROFESSIONAL TO COME TO ENGLAND).

5th.	DEC.	1885	STAVELY	STAVELY	1--2	
16th.	APRIL	1898	DERBY CO.	CRYSTAL PALACE	3--1.	capes 2. mcpherson 1.

NOTTINGHAM FOREST
THE
EARLY DAYS.

MATCH REPORTS.

V. WOLVERHAMPTON STAFFORD ROAD WORKS
FEBRUARY 17th. and FEBRUARY 24th. 1882

V. WEDNESBURY OLD ATHLETIC
MARCH 10th. and MARCH 17th.1882

V. STOKE.
MARCH 26th. 1883

V. NOTTS COUNTY
OCTOBER 20th. 1883

V. DUMBARTON
NOVEMBER 27th. 1883

V. STAVELY
DECEMBER 12th. 1885

V. WEST BROMWICH

MAY 19TH. 1883

V. DERBY COUNTY

APRIL 16th. 1898

NOTTINGHAM FOREST
THROUGH THE EYES
OF THE FAMOUS RED
Dr. TINSLEY LINDLEY

ALSO
SOME EARLY DAYS
OF THE
ENGLAND TEAM

NOTTINGHAM FOREST v WOLVERHAMPTON STAFFORD ROAD WORKS FEBRUARY 17th, 1882 AT THE STAFFORD ROAD GROUND

In the presence of but a small sprinkling of spectators, the above match took place at the Stafford Road Ground, Wolverhampton on Saturday afternoon, the weather was fine overhead but there was a keen north wind blowing the whole time, whilst then somewhat contrary to exception, the contest proved very tame and one sided as from the first to the last, even when playing with a strong wind in their favour, the home side were hopelessly out matched and at call of time the Forest had scored 6 goals to 1, despite the superiority of the visitors however, the Wolves played a remarkable plucky, and at times creditable game, their passing was good but they lacked coolness at the critical moment and seldom succeeded in persuading the Forest back to allow the leather to get behind them.

Two well known faces were missing in the composition of the reds eleven, Viz, Harp and Caborn both of whom are still suffering from injuries received in the recent match against Blackburn Rovers, the vacancies thus being occasionalised were supplied by Barlow and Tinsley Lindley, both of whom are doubtedly "Coming Men", for sometime past Lindley has been recognised as one who was as it were, a born footballer, hitherto, however due to his youth, has only come under public notice as a prominent member of the Forest 2nd team and as captain of the high school team, but no matter with whom or where has has played, never once has he failed to prominently distinguish himself, on Saturday it was his play alone that presented, his cool and collected demeaner, a perfect knowledge of strict adhesion distinctly mark him as more than a valuable addition to the future Forest team, with commendable punctuality, both took up their positions and Widdowson having won the toss, kicked off against the wind, the leather was quickly taken into the home sides territory, but when strangely enough the most favourable opportunity that the Wolverhampton have had of scoring during the whole afternoon was fruitlessly thrown away, play then became central, until Widdowson awaiting his opportunity secures a capital run giving the

Forest the first corner, from which however nothing resulted, the leather now took up residence in the home sides quarter, and for some little time neither the herculean efforts of the backs, nor even the strong wind that was blowing, were effectual in persuading a departure, Widdowson and Danks soon drew first blood, whilst Lindley continually exercised the nimbleness of the besieged keeper, soon after the first score Billyeald scored a second, whilst corner kicks were the order of the day and before half-time a third goal was added, the second half of the game was very tame, during the one-sided play that ensued, Lindley scored three more goals for the Forest and just before the finish the home side managed to rush the leather through the posts.

Wolverhampton Stafford Road Works 1 v Nottingham Forest 6

Wolverhampton Team	Nottingham Forest Team
Phillips	J. Sands
J. Nicholls	E. Luntley
H. Crump	T. Hancock
A. Nicholls	Barlow
W. Richards	H. Billyeald
J. Baker	S. Norman
Walter	S. Danks
J. Richards	H. Fletcher
F. Deacon	S. Widdowson (capt.)
O. Foster	W. Parr
R. Gowland	T. Lindley

NOTTINGHAM FOREST v
WOLVERHAMPTON STAFFORD ROAD WORKS
FEBRUARY 24th, 1882 AT THE
TRENT BRIDGE GROUND, NOTTINGHAM

A match between teams representing the above football clubs was played on the Trent Bridge Ground in Nottingham on Saturday afternoon last, in the presence of a comparatively small number of spectators and resulted in a decided victory for the home team by six goals to nil, the strangers won the toss, Widdowson kicked off for the Forest in a rather strong wind at ten minutes to four o'clock, after some kicking in the middle of the field, a corner kick was awarded to the Forest, the ball quickly carried to the other end, but Hancock prevented the strangers from scoring, Parr and Widdowson then dribbled well on the right and Parr made a shot for goal, the ball landing right in front, then Danks kicked it through, thus making the first goal from the Forest, the Forest goalkeeper "Sands" had to handle and Parr and Widdowson again distinguished themselves, making a brilliant run between them, but Lindley kicked the ball over, Fletcher soon after made a good shot at goal, but Phillips knocked the ball back with his head, a corner kick was then got by the Wolverhampton team, but the ball was kicked behind the post, hands was given against the strangers about five yards out from their goal, Widdowson kicked off and a corner kick was given, a foul was afterwards given against the strangers and Billy Eald who kicked off, sent the ball between the posts without touching any of the players, another corner kick was got by the Forest, Norman kicked the ball well in front, and Bullyeald made a shot for goal, the ball struck Phillips hands and passed through thus securing the second goal for the Forest, Widdowson then made a shot, but the keeper, knocking the ball back, a good chance of scoring was lost through the other players not supporting Widdowson, another shot was made by Lindley but the keeper kicked the ball back out and Widdowson sent it through thus making it a third goal to none, as half-time was called, Deacon kicked off after the teams had changed ends, after three or four narrow escapes Lindley made an attempt to score, the ball hit the crossbar and rebounded back, the same player scored the fourth goal, two corner kicks were got on the left by the Forest but nothing came of them, a corner kick was taken by Sands, who had exchanged places with Danks at half-time, but Lindley knocked the ball over the line with his head, soon after Lindley succeeded in obtaining the 5th goal for the Forest, four corner kicks followed for Forest the first on the left and the others on the right, when the last was taken the ball was sent right in front of the goal, Widdowson fell over the ball and Lindley kicked it through, making it six goals to none, the ball was then for the first time in the second half of the game carried close to the Forest, another corner was awarded, their 13th as against their one.

Nottingham Forest 6 v Wolverhampton Stafford Road Works 0

Nottingham Forest Team	Wolverhampton Team
J. Sands	Phillips
E. Luntley	J. Nicholls
T. Hancock	H. Crump
H. Billyeald	A. Nicholls
Barlow	J. Richards
S. Norman	J. Baker
S. Danks	W. Richards
S. Widdowson (capt.)	O. Foster
W. Parr	R. Gowland
T. Lindley	H. Turton

Referee: H. Davis   Umpires: W. Grant and A. T. Grant

NOTES

Forest had almost as easy task with the Wolves club Stafford Road Works, as the Notts experienced with their antagonists from Birmingham, A. J. Caborn and Earp were both absent on the side of the reds their places being filled by A. Barlow and T. Lindley, the latter player is only 16 years of age, but the Forest are to be congratulated on the possession of one who shows so much ability, and so great a promise of future excellence, he filled the position of centre forward, which throughout the season has been one weak spot of the Forest team but it must have been a source of much gratification to the older members of the club that the latest addition to the ranks of the first eleven obtained for his side 3 of the 6 goals which were scored, the match at Trent Bridge hardly permits of much lengthened comment, the home club simply played the Stafford Road off the field, and if it had been at all necessary could probably have added more to their total they made, the losers have made no advance since last winter of 1880-1881, when, as stated last week they defeated Aston Villa by 3 goals to 2, only to be beaten in the 4th round by the Old Etonians who won a good game by 2 goals to 0 on Saturday last, however, they made no headway against the Forest who were victorious by 6 goals to 1, so far as individual players on the side of the winners were concerned E. Luntley, Caborn, Billy Eald, Parr and Fletcher all played exceedingly well, and the way in which the wearer's of the red jersey have once more returned to their best form is not the least remarkable of the present season.

WEDNESBURY NATIONAL CHARITY CUP MATCH
NOTTINGHAM FOREST v WEDNESBURY OLD ATHLETIC
MARCH 10th, 1882 CASTLE CLUB GROUND, NOTTINGHAM

On November 25th. the above teams met at the Trent Bridge Ground to play off their match in the 1st. round of ties in the Wednesbury National Charity Cup competition the fixture ended in a draw with the score of 4 goals each, but owing to the refusal of the Wednesbury team to continue the game for an extra half-hour, the tie was claimed by the Nottingham Forest club, after much correspondence and a lengthened postponement it was finally decided to play the match again, preparations for the cricket season being active at the Trent Bridge ground, it was arranged to bring off the game at the Castle Club ground, and this having been swept of the snow which fell on Thursday, it might have afforded a better field of play than might have been expected under the circumstances, some 1200 spectators assembled to witness the game, which however, robbed of much interest by weak sides which represented both clubs, on the side of the Forest, Caborn. Luntley and Widdowson were all away, while on the side of the visitors, the brothers Holdens, 2 of their best players were absentees, owing to accidents in a match against West Brom, J. Cliffe from a similar cause was also unable to play, and the majority of those who did duty for the club, were second team men, the ground was somewhat heavy and slippery, anything like really good play being out of the question, Forest won the toss and at 5 minutes past 3 the visitors kicked off the game, for a minute or two in the home teams end, but when Forest had settled down to their work they began to press their antagonism, a corner kick fell to the Notts men Kent had to twice use his hands, the proceedings were even character, each goal in turn being attacked and though neither clubs acquitted themselves particularly well, the respective custodians showed some capital defence, especially where the state of the ground is taken into consideration, once when Kent fell, a point should have been scoredby the Nottingham men, but the play of the forwards was weak in the extreme, Nicholls and Whitehouse managing to get the ball out of danger, at last Lindley gained possession in the centre and making a splendid dodging run through his opponents scored a capital goal for the Forest, for a short time little movement occurred until Wednesbury secured a corner kick, but could make nothing of it, while Parr and Lindley in turn looked very threatening the last named sending in a shot which just went on the wrong side of the post, another corner fell to Forest but was fruitless, while after a change of ends, a persisted attack on the Wednesbury position ended in the ball being shot over the cross-bar, a fine run by Woodcock began on the left close to the red posts, a shot being missed and just saved on the goal-line by Sands, Wednesbury claimed a goal which was allowed by the referee, and after Hancock twice kicked behind his own line, the corners were both unproductive, and from this point to the call of time, the Notts men had much the best of the proceedings Billyeald played exceedingly well and corner after corner was taken by the Forest men, but Kent worked very hard between the posts and managed to preserve his charge intact, Sands also saved a splendid shot sent in by Woodcock, but the hour and a half originally fixed with only one goal to the credit of each side, though the Forest have had 8 corners to 3 obtained by their opponents, the match having again ending in a tie, it was mutually decided to continue for an extra half-hour, 15 minutes from each goal, it was plainly evident that the home team had fairly worn down their antagonists, for when play was resumed Parr made a pretty run down the right wing and centering to Fletcher the player quickly scored the second goal for his side, another corner was taken by the Forest and though the Wednesbury forwards got the ball away it was quickly turned and from a pass by Parr, Lindley obtained possession and shot the ball between the visitors posts for the third goal, when the teams changed ends Lindley took the ball down to the Wednesbury goal, Fletcher badly missing a chance of further increasing the reds score, while Sands had to be quick to repel an attack from Woodcock, the side gained another corner, but towards the conclusion of the proceedings were exceedingly tame, the Forest eventually winning by 5 goals to 1, for the home team Billyeald was perhaps the best player, while Sands, Hancock and Lindley were also prominent, for their exertions, Woodcock, Kent and Nicholls worked hard for the visitors.

Nottingham Forest 5 v Wednesbury Old Athletic 1

Nottingham Forest Team	Wednesbury Old Athletic
J. Sands	Kent
T. Hancock	J. Nicholls (capt.)
Taylor	R. Whitehouse
H. Billyeald	R. Mason
S. Norman	J. Shenton
E .Luntley	H. Wood
Fletcher	A. Woodcock
Danks	A. Price
T. Lindley	W. Whitehouse
Earp (capt.)	A. Cliffe
Parr	J. Cliffe

Referee: F. B. Montague (London Athletic Club)

Umpires: E. Jardine and J. Taylor

THE WEDNESBURY NATIONAL CHARITY CUP TIE
NOTTINGHAM FOREST v WEDNESBURY OLD ATHLETIC
MARCH 17th, 1882 KICK-OFF 3pm ATTENDANCE 2,000
AT THE CASTLE CLUB GROUND, NOTTINGHAM

This match, being in connection in a tie with the above Charity Cup, was played on the Castle Club Ground on Saturday last, in the presence of nearly 2,000 spectators, there was not much interest in the match, but those present were doubtless pleased to see excellent form shown by the reds who however were far from being strongly represented, the game was very even indeed, the home team, if anything, showing a little superior speed, and at the call of time, each team was credited with one goal, in the extra half-hour play, which was agreed upon by the reds had an opportunity of asserting their superiority, and won a good match by 3 goals to 1, the Forest have a good chance of winning the cup.

The visitors kicked off at 3.05pm, towards the town, the ground was very slippery, as a consequence of recent snowstorms and as a matter of course, fast was almost out of the question, Earp on the left, they obtained a corner for Forest and a change resulted, but it was successful and the ball afterwards frequently out of play, a good shot by Earp, but the Wednesbury goalkeeper came out to handle and it was from another long shot by the same player passed over the cross-bar, then this time considering the state of the ground, play was good, and in turn Sands was compelled to prevent the visitors making a goal by Woodcock, but Sands was equal to the occasion and nothing resulted, the leather was then worked in the visitors territory and from a throw-in Lindley scored for the home team, after the ball had seen action for 23 minutes, Parr, Norman and Danks distinguished themselves, and the latter nearly scored, in passing the ball to the immediate left of the Wednesbury goal, the corner that followed was unsaved and several shots were made at goal, but were saved, at half-time the reds possessed the play, but on the game being resumed, the visitors scored and equalised matters, an objection on off-side was made but disallowed, the game equally divided, a call of time was called, both had played very well, it was decided to play an extra half-hour and then the reds soon assumed and Parr, to whom the ball was passed to made a second goal, the score was extended by another from the foot of Danks, the visitors after many attempts failed to score, but there was an expiration of time, and the home team won by 3 goals to 1.

Nottingham Forest Team	Wednesbury Old Athletic
J. Sands	Kent
T. Hancock	A. Cliffe
H. Norman	Price
E. Luntley	A. Woodcock
H. Billyeald	F. Mason
F. Earp (capt.)	J. Cliffe
T. Lindley	R. Whitehouse
Fletcher	H. Wood
Danks	J. Shenton
W. Parr	W. Whitehouse
Taylor	J. Nicholls

Referee: F. B. Montague   Umpires: Mr. J. Taylor

STOKE v NOTTINGHAM FOREST
MARCH 26th, 1883   KICK-OFF 2.15pm   ATTENDANCE: 600
AT STOKE

The 2nd in a series of matches was played at Stoke on Monday afternoon in the presence of about 600 spectators, owing to the recent snowstorms and continued thaw, the ground was in a wretched state, the consequence was the heaviest team had the advantage, at 2.15, Johnson having lost the toss kicked off from the North End with the sun in his face, it was evident from the first that the Forest teams superior weight told very much against the lightweight physique of the Stoke men, the play was very even for the first half-hour, Johnson did a brilliant run occasionally, but to no purpose, being badly supported, his men seemed to play very lazily and without much spirit, the Forest men pressed Stoke very much for the last quarter of an hour before half-time and scored 3 goals, on ends changed the local team faired still worse, and the Forest scored 4 more goals in good form. With the exception of an occasional run, the Stoke man could do very little, the

Forest scored 4 more goals and all the play seemed to have gone out of them, when Johnson, about 5 minutes before call of time and by an exceptionally brilliant run passed the Forest backs and scored the first goal for Stoke, this seemed to put a little life into the game, and in an incredibly short time Johnson did another run and passed to Myatt who centred well, some very exciting play took place right in the Forest goal, the ball rebounding into play twice from the goal-posts, the Forest goalkeeper defended his charge admirably, but the Stoke men were not to be denied, and amidst tremendous applause, Bennett kicked a second goal for Stoke just before the call of time, for Stoke, Johnson, Stanford, Bennett, Miller and Bettany played the best, while Ringland and Myatt played indifferently, for the Forest, Parr, Widdowson, Lindley, Earp and the backs showed best form.

Stoke 2 v Nottingham Forest 11

Stoke	Nottingham Forest
Wilden	W. Luntley
Mellor	Ward
Ringland	Hancock
Stanford	Norman
Bettany	H. Billyeald
Johnson	Parr
Bennett	Widdowson
Shutt	Lindley
Myatt	Earp
Brown	E. Luntley
Fennel	Fletcher

Referee: H. Allen Umpire: E. Oliver

THE WEDNESBURY NATIONAL CHARITY CUP FINAL
WEST BROMWICH ALBION v NOTTINGHAM FOREST
MAY 19th, 1883 KICK-OFF 4pm ATTENDANCE: 2500
AT PERRY BARR, BIRMINGHAM

West Brom	Nottingham Forest
Roberts	Sands
T. Bell	Hancock
Stanton	Luntley
White (capt.)	H. Billyeald
Horton	Norman
G. Bell	Earp (capt.)
Timmins	Fletcher
Bissiker	Lindley
Whitehouse	Parr
Bunns	Barlow
Aston	Taylor

Referee: Mr. Crump, (A Wolves player)

No club within our remembrance of midland football has come so rapidly to the front as the most deservedly favourite black country team, who this afternoon did battle for the possession of the "Wednesbury Charity Trophy" with Nottingham Forest, even our own "Villa" with all their swift ascension of fame, cannot in this respect claim premier honours to "Don Juan" of the athlete, undoubtedly has to the cried of first attracting attention to the clever little players who had from the abode of "Siders" Bob Roberts, Bell and Ironside of the puddles district, were hardly heard of beyond their own town until commencement of last season and before the conclusion they had worked their way right into the final quartette of clubs for the Birmingham Cup Competition and fallen no easy prey than to the Wednesbury Athletic who just managed to head them by one point, after a most exciting tussle, we remember well, being in West Bromwich one Saturday right before the final ties were drawn, and hearing a member of the team express a hope that they might be coupled with the Villa, we know we should be beaten modestly said he. But they would play us a good game, the present season the "Perry Pets" are not the only Birmingham and District Club who can play a good game, their achievements during the last 6 months were too well known to need commenting on, the Villa were decidedly caught on the hop during a time when for a few weeks they were all together off colour, the crushing disposal of the Walsall Cup holders by 5 goals to 1, was good evidence as to their form and as everybody knows they are not at the present time holders of the handsome pot put up by the Staffordshire Association.

The Foresters have been too frequent visitors to Birmingham, not to be well known and admitted, there is no team in existence we should think who have suffered more from persistent bad luck than the celebrated Nottingham Reds, some months ago they were admittedly the first eleven bar none in the provinces and how the varsity managed that into business is one of those things no fellish can understand, in a plato presented some time ago to readers of a London contempory of the famous English football players, 4 out of 5 portraits given were of Nottingham Forest celebrities, Widdowson and Luntley are household names to the leather fraternity and where will you find a grander goalkeeper than Sands.

Once before they made a bid for the self same cup, losing in the semi-final against "Old Athletic" at Wednesbury by 4 goals to 1, this defeat has been a little softened down by knocking out of the hunt some weeks ago by 4 goals to 3, after playing extra time at Nottingham, injustice to the Wednesbury men let it be said, that several of their best players were not on the field, bearing 2 such names than as these two organisations do. A first class encounter was of course expected by the numerous assembly gathered round the Perry Bar enclosure this afternoon, much speculation was rife as to the result, the black country partisans very unnaturally fearing that the magnificent defence invariably presented by the Foresters great back division would prove too much even for the nimble little Albion skirmishers, the weather was everything that could be desired as a matter of course, the black country element formed an important portion of spectators.

Lindley at about 5 minutes past 4pm started the leather uphill and after a few seconds, midfield passing was the thing, Parr and Barlow got possession and eventually landed a corner and Lindley nearly scored a beauty, G. Bell at last getting hold, had a fine opening on the left, the backs being up the field, Billyeald steadying himself, cooly shot straight across the goalmouth Aston spurting just caught the sphere on the hop and before Sands could possibly interfere in anyway the West Bromwich men were a goal to the good, 3 minutes from the start, an appeal for offside was disallowed and Lindley at once, restarting the Notts again forced the ball into rival territory, where for some minutes it remained, Timmins and Bell endeavoured to get away, but were repulsed by Billyeald again capturing the ball, the Nottingham players in a second or two were crowding round the black country stronghold, after very effective heading and at last skulled it past Roberts, who seemed to us to have ruined and easy shot, one goal each. Bissiker restarted and each team playing more carefully, nothing of any note occurred, for a few minutes, except once, when Roberts fisted out an excellent try by Parr, the visitors, if anything having the best of it, Bissiker attempted to change the venue of play, but Norman intervened, G. Bell in having a twist ran the ball out, at this period the game was very even and confined chiefly to midfield, at last Whitehouse and Aston bowled down the right, and a serious bombardment of the Forest citadel nearly resulted in its capture, only for the excellent heading of Hancock and Taylor missing a score, a short visit to the top goal and G. Bell, dodging in pretty style, completely did Norman and getting well down his wing made a splendid screw across the goal, but Aston smartly returning the leather, the Albion were again a point ahead, from kick-off the Notts made straight for their opposite goal, Barlow putting it out, Sands was forced to run out and save his charge, in the next minute repeating the dose, a little afterwards, some very long kicking was now indulged by both sides until the Forest left's made off with it up to the top end where gaining a corner they looked like scoring but it came to nothing, although Roberts was obliged to punch out a shot of Parry, which he did in praiseworthy style Lindley going for him, each side seemed to be trying each-others strength and dashing runs and brilliant dodging were conspicuous only by it's absence. Horton went in directly after some decent tackling and Bell relieved the monotony by making a good run, and a bad shot the wrong side of the posts, Bissiker, not to be outdone landed the ball right out through the wings, when a fine chance in front of goal was missed, the Forest boss and his partner Fletcher were stopped in a very promising run by call of a foul, this was given against them, the captain out of revenge, we suppose, banging the ball past the posts a few inches the wrong side, a foul against the Albion was the next feature, Whitehouse rushed off down the wing, the other 4 backing him up well, but Lindley very diplomatically put the leather out, a feat for which he was prodigiouly hooted, Hancock a minute afterwards kicked it out, but nothing came of it, and it glided smoothly on, the players seemed to feel the heat and we ourselves on the reporters benches began to experience symptoms of solemness, Aston at last woke us up by a first class run down the right, doing Luntley and Billyeald with ease the goalkeeper out, Aston shot, somebodies head got in the way, Taylor bumped it up field, and a rare chance was lost, but Aston was not done with yet, again getting possession performed the same trick again and Sands hands threw it out, G. Bell eventually having a go to smash up the Villa goalposts, the cheers so far the best of the afternoon had scarcely died away when call of time was called, with the score standing at Albion 2 Forest 1.

On the restart the Nottingham men pressed the Albion severely on several occasions, having hard lines in not scoring, after some ten minutes Aston and Whitehouse getting possession were favoured with an excellent opening, but the former player shot wildly across to the opposite wing, where it was lost, the leather again meandered to the Wellington Road end goal, where after a little mild excitement Lindley obtained a goal, which proved to be an offside one, Aston again spurted off up the field and Sands who had been playing sort of mixed half-three quarter back and a good game returned to his charge rather briskly, and Luntley and Billy Eald went down before the crack West Brom right, but Hancock was all there and from his kick the Foresters took the leather right down to the Albion goalmouth, the ball being at last spooned over the bar, (hard lines) again to the Forest, the lacers swarmed round Freemans fortress, Lindley making the game even, a swift run by Parr was nipped in the bud by the Albion, but the reds returning directly to the assault, a scrimmage occurred, and amid much cheering the ball was rushed through the posts, the Nottingham men were now one goal ahead. The Albion were now decidedly having the worst yet, Roberts on one occasion officiating in magnificent style in goal, black country faces could now very nearly be seen to lengthen as shot after shot was hurled at the West Brom stronghold, Aston rousing himself to the situation put in a desperate run, leaving his opponents well behind him a goal seemed certain but instead of shooting, he passed across and the chance was lost, Earp and Fletcher returned the complement on the right and touching it over smartly to the centre, the Notts forwards again rushed it through, the Albion now seemed disheartened, Hortons unique defence alone being seen as an advantage. A few minutes out remained to play, when after a sharp run Whitehouse passed to Bissiker who scored again for the Albion.

Notts 4 Albion 3, another short burst by Aston and the Notts coming away in fine style put it through for the 5th time, before the ball could be restarted time was called, it is only fair to say that the Albion played a man short nearly all the last half, Whitehouse was injured soon after half-time, the Notts thus won the final tie for the Wednesbury Charity Cup 1882-1883, by 5 goals to 3. This was the first cup the Forest have won, to take to the Maypole Yard, Nottingham.

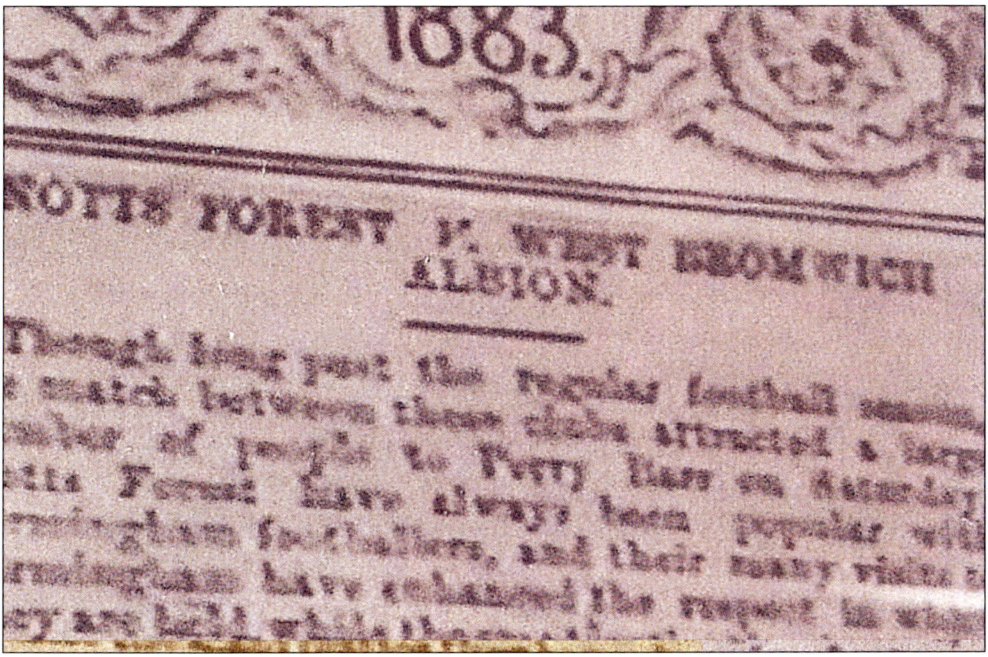
1883.

NOTTS FOREST V. WEST BROMWICH ALBION.

WEST BROMWICH ALBION 1883

1883

THE WEDNESBURY NATIONAL CHARITY CUP.

Way back in the 1800s
In the year of 83
Nottingham Forest football team
Won the Wednesbury Cup you see

It was against West Brom the Albion
And the score was 5 to 3
They played the match at Perry Bar
Over in the Black Country

It was the first cup the Forest have won
And it was a joyous time
To take it back to the Maypole Yard
And drink some lovely wine

The team it was as follows
There was Sands he was in goal
Hancock and Taylor were the backs
And in the middle Huntley showed

By the side of him the half-backs
Captain Earp and Norman too
In front of them came Lindley
A goalscorer oh so true

On the attacking front with him was Barlow
Inside to him was Parr
That completes the lineup
For the Forest stars

Now we come to the West Brom
A team they say as good
Between the posts came Roberts
A goalie and tall he stood

In front of him came Stanton
Horton, Timmins and Bell
Bissiker and Bunns were in the front
And Whitehouse was playing well

The man Aston could bolt
And the umpires Scott and Holt
H. Crump was the ref, and he kept his head
He blew his whistle with the Forest ahead.

Written by Ron Clarke February 2008

NOTTS COUNTY v NOTTINGHAM FOREST
OCTOBER 20th, 1883 KICK-OFF 3.14pm ATTENDANCE: 4000 plus
AT PARKSIDE GROUND, NOTTINGHAM

For the first time this season the two chief local football clubs met on Saturday afternoon on the Forest's new ground, Parkside and the match ended in a draw, neither team being able to score a goal, the match had been looked forward to with great interest, and the consequence was that the spectators numbered considerably more than 4000, a large proportion of them being ladies, the game was a very fast one, and exceedingly rough, many of the players getting bad falls, the number of claims made by each side for one thing or another was also very large and taking everything into consideration, it was fortunate perhaps that a stranger Mr. Liddle of Sheffield acted as referee, both teams were fairly represented and when their full strength was seen, and exceedingly keen and close game was looked upon as a certainty, the Forest players were first to appear at 4 minutes past 3, and their opponents followed after an interval of 8 minutes, Venables the county captain lost the toss, and the Forest chose the Derby End of the ground thus being on a slightly higher level, the wind blew across, so that it favoured neither side, Venables who played in the centre during the first half, started the leather at 14 minutes past 3 and it was kept at close proximity to the county clubs goal for a considerable time, Fox was the first player who could attempt to score, but MaCrae stopped the ball in splendid style, Widdowson had another attempt, but also failed, Earp then dribbled well on the left, and afterwards made a well judged shot at the Notts fortress, the ball passing his opponents within a foot of the goalpost, Fox on the right then showed his move to advantage successfully passing his opponents and then giving Widdowson a good chance which he failed to take, a foul was given in favour of Forest and Fox kicked well for goal, but Sherwin knocked the ball back with his fist, another foul was given to Notts and Fox caused Sherwin to handle a second time, the ball for the first time was taken to the other end of the ground and Venables nearly scored, Fox then brought the leather to the Notts part of the ground again and passed to Widdowson who however failed to score, although he has a fairly good opportunity, Smith followed with a good run on the right, but the ball was kicked over the boundary and quickly returned to the other end of the ground, where again Fox caused Sherwin to handle, H. Cursham than had a long run on the Notts right and shot for goal, but W. Luntley preserved his charge, MaCrae however got possession and made another attempt causing Luntley to handle, Fox again played well on the right, tackling Gunn successfully, but the Notts backs averted danger, Fox soon had possession of the leather again and passed it to Earp, that player then made a well judged pass over Sherwins head, he however was equal to the occasion and stepping back over the boundary, knocked the ball back with his arm, claim was made for a goal on the part of the Forest team, but was disallowed, corner kick for Notts was kicked behind the posts, Earp then played well on the Forest left and was ably supported by Widdowson who had another good chance, but he kicked the ball against the cross-bar, 2 corner kicks were won by the Forest players within a very short time of each other, but nothing resulted from it, after a good run on the right by Gunn, hands were given against Notts and a corner kick for Forest was taken by Earp, the ball however kicked over the bar, in a rally in front of Sherwins charge, Earp passed the ball to Lindley who further passed it to Widdowson, that player did not kick with sufficient force, and Sherwin was able to stop the ball with ease, a corner kick which followed was taken by Fox on the right, but Smith carried it and passed to Earp who was ably assisted by Fletcher and those players gave Billyeald a chance, but S. MaCrae amidst great excitement carried the ball away in grand style, soon after Gunn and Fox tried conclusions, first one player getting the advantage then the other, Gunn and MaCrae in conjunction, afterwards played exceedingly well, but Earp, Fletcher and Lindley succeeded in taking the ball close to the Notts goal, but a foul was given against the Forest, Luntley's charge was then closely besieged but all attempts upon it were rendered futile through the excellent play of the backs, soon after Sherwin was obliged to handle in consequence of the ball a good shot by Fox, after some good play on the part of H. Cursham, Moore, MaCrae and Gunn the ball was returned to the Notts goal and Widdowson had a good chance but failed to score, Sherwin prevented Earp from scoring again, and hands were given against the Notts in front of their own goal, there were claims for hands against Notts again when the first 45 minutes had terminated, after the interval, Hancock stopped a good run made by Venables who now played on the right wing,

H. A. Cursham having taken his usual position as the centre forward, after a foul by Forest, Sherwin had to handle again to prevent Fletcher from scoring, after some good play by Lindley and Widdowson for the Forest and by Emmett and Cursham for their opponents, Earp made a well judged shot for goal, but Sherwin again returned it with his fist, a corner kick for Forest followed on the left, but Earp kicked the ball over the boundary, soon after the Notts team pressed the Forest very hard, Luntley having to handle, Hancock was very useful as a back, stopping good runs made by the Notts players he also stopped the ball which had been well aimed at goal by Smith, Gunn then caused Luntley to handle and Earp succeeded in taking the ball to the other end of the field, the Dobsons however returned it to their forwards and Caborn took it from Gunn, Smith then kicked it high above the goal-posts, Lindley then tackled 2 Notts players with success and passed the ball to Earp who made an unsuccessful shot for goal, MaCrae had a long run with the ball and went close to the Forest goal, it was passed to H. Cursham, but Hancock kicked away, hands were given against Cursham to the Forest goal but the ball was quickly returned by Moore, H. A. Cursham however kicked it over the boundary, MaCrae soon got possession of the leather again, and passed it to Gunn, who failed in an attempt to give H. Cursham an opportunity of scoring, the ball was then passed over the line close to the Notts goal, Venables brought it down the ground, but Hancock stopped him, Smith and Cursham also failed in another attempt that followed Luntley however having to handle, Venables had an excellent run on the right and passed the ball right in front of the Forest goal, but the other forwards were too far away, and a very good chance was lost, soon after H. Cursham made a good shot for goal, but the ball passed just above the bar, Barlow had just the ball from Venables when time was called, the game thus ending in a draw.

No goals were gotten by either side. As a rule all players played well individually, but Lindley's play was rather disappointing following his exhibition against Sheffield Town on Saturday where he scored 6 goals. Sherwin's goalkeeping was faultless and Luntley also deserved commendation.

Notts County 0 v Nottingham Forest 0

Notts County	Nottingham Forest
M. Sherwin	W. Luntley
A. T. Dobson	C. J. Caborn
H. Emmett	S. Norman
C. F. Dobson	H. Billy Eald
S. MaCrae	E. Barlow
E. Harker	F. Fox
R. H. Venables	S. Widdowson
S. G. Smith	T. Lindley
H. Cursham	H. S. Fletcher
A. E. Moore	F. W. Earp
W. M. Gunn	W. F. Hancock

Referee: Mr. Liddle (Sheffield) Umpires: Mr. Sands & Mr. Jessop

THE FOLLOWING TABLE SHOWS RESULTS OF MATCHES SINCE THEIR INSTITUTION IN 1878

Nottingham Forest v Notts County

November 16th,	1878	Beeston	Forest won 3-1
November 8th,	1879	Trent Bridge	Forest won 4-0
January 17th,	1880	Trent Bridge	Forest won 7-1
December 16th,	1880	Trent Bridge	Forest won 1-0
March 6th,	1881	Castle Ground	Notts County won 1-0
December 17th,	1881	Trent Bridge	Notts County won 5-0
March	1882	Castle Ground	Forest won 2-1
January 20th,	1883	Trent Bridge	Draw
October 20th,	1883	Parkside	Draw

NOTTINGHAM FOREST v DUMBARTON
NOVEMBER 27th, 1883 KICK-OFF 2.45pm ATTENDANCE: 3000 plus
AT THE PARKSIDE GROUND, LENTON, NOTTINGHAM

A team representing the most famous 'Dumbarton' Football Club, the present holders of the Scottish Challenge Cup met the Nottingham Forest on the ground of the latter at the Parkside, Lenton on Saturday afternoon, after one of the most exciting as well as one of the finest games ever played in Nottingham, the Scotsmen came off victors with 3 goals to 2, it maybe mentioned here that this was the first defeats sustained by the Foresters during the present season as yet, previous to Saturday last they had played 7 matches of which they had won 6 and drew 1 with Notts County on the 27th October the clubs defeated were Small Heath Alliance, Wednesbury Stroller, Stoke-on-Trent, Nottingham Swifts and Sheffield Attercliffe, the prowess of the Dumbarton men is too well known to require the recapitulation of their success, but it might be mentioned that they beat the Queen's Park, 3 weeks ago by 3 goals to 1, the number of spectators on Saturday was very large, somewhere in the region of 3000, but still not nearly so large as was present at the match between the great local rivals 5 weeks ago, play was advertised to commence at 2.30pm and Dumbartonites were the first to enter the area, a few minutes after that time they were followed by the Forest representatives almost immediately afterwards, and it was soon to be seen there were two international players in the team, A. McCauley and W. McKinnon, the goalkeeper and left back.

The Scotch captain won the toss and chose the Derby Road End of the ground, thus playing up hill and against a slight wind, during the first 45 minutes S. W. Widdowson kicked off for the home team at 2.45pm, a slight shower of rain falling at the time, which however only continued for a few minutes and the weather was all that could be desired during the rest of the game, the condition of the ground was also about as good as was possible for the Parkside ground to be in, after the commencement of play Lindley and Widdowson succeeded in working the ball towards the Scotchmen's goal and passed to Fox who made a well judged shot, but McCauley stopped it with ease, and kicked the sphere to the middle of the field, the 2 browns made a rapid charge up the right passing on the wrong side of the post, Earp nearly carried the ball into the stranger's quarters but a foul was given against Sam

Widdowson, and the 2 Brown's again ran away with the ball on the right wing, R. Brown (1) made another clever shot, which caused Luntley to handle, Brown won again (1) made another attempt, which was also repulsed and one of the centres headed the ball forward, but Luntley again saved this charge, 2 fouls against each team followed very quickly, and then R. Brown (2) sent in so clever a shot and was ably supported by the centres, then Luntley was forced to knock the ball over the boundary, thus giving the strangers a corner which was taken on the right by R. Brown (2) landed the ball well in front of goal, in a scrimmage which ensued, another corner was given to the Scotch team, A. Brown (2) also took that corner and place the ball at the feet of L. Keir, who cleverly sent the ball between the posts, just 15 minutes from the start, the point was appealed against by the Foresters because they considered that Keir was offside, and also that the goalkeeper was charged, but the ref disallowed the claim, the reds then played more plucky than ever, but for sometime they were unable to pass the Scotch backs, Hutchinson and McKinnon who were playing a magnificent game, at last Fletcher worked the ball into the neighbourhood of the goal, when hands were given against one of the Dumbarton backs, Billyeald took the free-kick and cleverly passed to Lindley who shot for goal, but the ball struck the cross-bar and rebounded, and before anyone else could touch it Widdowson headed the ball between the posts amidst utmost excitement 22 minutes from the commencement, the score having thus equalised the game became more and more interesting and the attention of the spectators became more and more engrossed in the play, Fox and Widdowson were very conspicuous on the right but Kerr succeeded in taking the ball from them, E. Barlow almost instantly afterwards gave Widdowson a splendid chance and that player lowered the colours of the Dumbarton mentor the 2nd time amidst loud and prolonged cheering from the excited spectators, several attacks were subsequently made on the Dumbarton stronghold but the 2 backs hardly allowed the ball to pass them again, the Browns had another of their magnificent runs on the right, and another foul was given against the Foresters half way between their goal and the left hand corner, R. Brown (2) very dexterously kicked off, and then a very severe struggle took place in the very mouth of Luntley's charge ultimately G. Hutton one of the centres evaded the goalkeeper and scored the second point for his side, the score again being equal 2-2, Fox then had a good run on the right and Kerr being unable to stop him, he shot at goal, but McCauley fisted out and Lindley kicked over the bar, from this stage of the game until half-time, the Forest pressed very severely and compelled to act on the defensive, but were unable to preserve their goal intact and when the teams changed ends, the score was equal, as the Dumbarton men had thus the same number of goals as the Forest when they were playing uphill and against the wind, which was however not very strong, it was confidently expected that the Forest would be defeated and this proved to be the case, a foul was given against Widdowson soon after the restart of play, Lindley then made a very good shot but McCauley fisted the leather out, Billyeald immediately returned it, and the goalkeeper again handled, a corner kick was gained by the Forest and was taken by Fox but McKinnon kicked the ball away and it was gradually worked up towards the Foresters stronghold in front of which a severe struggle ensued Luntley saved his charge once, but Brown (1), returned to the attack and succeeded in scoring the third goal for his side just five minutes after the interval, the same R. Brown soon after, made another attempt to score, but Luntley was equal to the occasion, a corner followed on the left for the Dumbarton, but Coville kicked behind the posts, hands were given against Caborn close to his own goal, but Hancock after the free kick had been taken sent the ball to the middle of the field, another corner was got by the Northerners, but nothing resulted from it, Earp than had a long run on the left and passed to Widdowson who in his turn neatly passed to Fox that player for goal, but the ball passed over the bar, Earp and Fletcher next attacked the Scotchmen's goal the backs returned the ball, hands were given against the Foresters and McKinnon took the free-kick, he kicked straight for goal from middle of the field and the ball passed between the posts without having been touched by any of the reds, ten minutes only remained and the light was rapidly failing, so that the progress of the game could not be properly seen, the play was however confined to the Forest end of the field, when time was called, no additional score had been gained, so that the game terminated in the favour of Dumbarton by 3 goals to 2, throughout the afternoon the Scotch players played a grand combination game and their splendid passing as well as their mode of defence were much to be admired, where every individual player did what he had to do in excellent manner, it is difficult to mention any names specially, but the 2 Browns, J. Keir, Hutchinson and McKinnon, appeared to be the most conspicuous, while the goalkeeping of McCauley was faultless, as for the Forest play, it could not have been much better and although defeated for only the first time this season it is a very honourable defeat, everyone did their very best, and the team may be considered to have acquitted themselves very satisfactorily against the champion club of Scotland.

Nottingham Forest	Dumbarton
W. Luntley	J. McCauley
C. J, Caborn	J. Hutchinson
Hancock	W. McKinnon
Norman	P. Miller
Billy Eald	L. Keir
Fox	R. Brown (1)
S. Widdowson	R. Brown (2)
T. Lindley	G. Hutton
Fletcher	A. Colville
Earp	A. Kennedy

Referee: J. A. Piggot (Derby)   Umpires: A. J, Bates & A. Kennedy

Tinsley Lindley with 2 of his cups

STAVELY v NOTTINGHAM FOREST
DECEMBER 12th, 1885 F.A. CUP ATTENDANCE: 2000

INTO THE STREET

This cup was a memorable one when we did battle with Stavely on their ground, memorable at least, if not to the present generation, I wonder what would happen now were a side to adopt the tactics that Stavely did on that occasion? the ground sloped steeply at one end and Stavely, kicking downhill led at the interval, with positions reversed, we got a goal and were pressing hard enough to pull the game out of the fire, when our opponents deliberately set themselves to kick the ball out of the ground, time after time it went into the adjoining street and although at least a quarter of an hour was wasted by those manoeuvres, the referee never added any time at the end of the game, in the end we were beaten by 2 goals to 1.

Nottingham Forest team:- Luntley, Caborn, Hancock, Ward, Norman, Billyeald, Widdowson, Leighton, Lindley, Unwin, Fox.

Referee:- Mr. Hames

FOOTBALL LEAGUE MEETING APRIL 15th, 1898

The league councillors on Friday, April 15th, 1898 held a meeting at Chancery Lane. W.C. The President Mr. J. J. Bentley occupied the chair.

There were also present:

J. Dunkley	(Aston Villa)
R. Molineaux	(Everton)
J. Parlby	(Manchester City)
W. H. Bellemy	(Grimsby)
H. Lockett	(Secretary)

Leicester Fosse were reported by Blackpool for having failed to pay the transfer fee for Keech, the money was ordered to be paid forthwith.

A claim was made by Luton Town against Newton-Heath for non-fulfilment of a league fixture, it was resolved that £63 4 shillings should be awarded by Newton-Heath to Luton Town as compensation, this being arrived at through taking the average gate at Luton in 6 league fixtures, less the amount taken on the day the match should have taken place.

Grimsby Town and Newton-Heath promised to arrange the question of their postponed match, failing which the matter will come before the league committee.

Derby County were asked to explain why they played a weak team against Everton, Bury and Preston-North-End. Nottingham Forest were asked the same with regard to their matches against Bury, Derby County and Bolton Wanderers and with respect to there games against Blackburn Rovers and Wolverhampton Wanderers.

THE ENGLISH CUP FINAL

16th APRIL 1898

CRYSTAL PALACE GROUND, LONDON

NOTTINGHAM FOREST

V

DERBY COUNTY

England FA Challenge Cup 1897-98

Jan 29	+Burnley	3	+Woolwich Arsenal	1	
Jan 29	Bury	1	Stoke	2	
Jan 29	Derby County	1	Aston Villa	0	
Jan 29	Everton	1	Blackburn Rovers	0	
Jan 29	Liverpool	2	*Hucknall St John	0	
Jan 29	*Long Eaton Rangers	0	+Gainsborough Trinity	1	
Jan 29	+Luton Town	0	Bolton Wanderers	1	
Jan 29	+Manchester City	1	*Wigan Borough	0	
Jan 29	+Newton Heath	1	+Walsall Town Swifts	0	
Jan 29	Nottingham Forest	4	+Grimsby Town	0	
Jan 29	Notts County	0	Wolverhampton Wanderers	1	
Jan 29	Preston North End	1	+Newcastle United	2	
Jan 29	**Sheffield United**	1	*Burslem Port Vale	1	
Jan 29	Southampton St Mary's	2	+Leicester Fosse	1	
Jan 29	Sunderland	0	The Wednesday	1	
Jan 29	West Bromwich Albion	2	*New Brighton Tower	0	
	Replay				
Feb 02	*Burslem Port Vale	2	**Sheffield United**	1	
	2nd Round				
Feb 12	Bolton Wanderers	1	+Manchester City	0	
Feb 12	+Burnley	3	*Burslem Port Vale	0	
Feb 12	+Newton Heath	0	Liverpool	0	
Feb 12	Nottingham Forest	4	+Gainsborough Trinity	0	
Feb 12	*Southampton St Mary's	1	+Newcastle United	0	
Feb 12	Stoke	0	Everton	0	
Feb 12	Wolverhampton Wanderers	0	Derby County	1	
Feb 12	West Bromwich Albion	1	The Wednesday	0	
	Replays				
Feb 16	Liverpool	2	+Newton Heath	1	
Feb 17	Everton	5	Stoke	1	
	Quarter-finals				
Feb 26	Bolton Wanderers	0	*Southampton St Mary's	0	
Feb 26	+Burnley	1	Everton	3	
Feb 26	Derby County	1	Liverpool	1	
Feb 26	West Bromwich Albion	2	Nottingham Forest	3	
	Replays				
Mar 02	Liverpool	1	Derby County	5	
Mar 02	*Southampton St Mary's	4	Bolton Wanderers	0	
	Semi-finals				
Mar 19	Derby County	3	Everton	1	played
Mar 19	Nottingham Forest	1	*Southampton St Mary's	1	played
	Replay				
Mar 24	Nottingham Forest	2	*Southampton St Mary's	0	played
	Final				
Apr 16	Nottingham Forest	3	Derby County	1	played

Football League Winners in Bold
+ 2nd Division Club
* Non-League Club

About this document

Prepared and maintained by *Macario Reyes Padilla* for the Rec.Sport.Soccer Statistics Foundation.

Author: Macario Reyes Padilla
Email: copasmundiales@igu.net,mx
Last updated: 28th January 2003

FOREST

AT THE

PALACE

16th.APRIL

1898

FOR MANY YEARS PAST

FOREST AND DERBY MATCH RECORDS

YEAR	DATE			FOREST GOALS	DERBY GOALS	
1885	January	31		1	6	
1885	April	6		1	1	
1885	December	5		2	1	
1886	January	9		0	1	
1887	February	19		2	2	
1887	March	12		2	1	
1888	November	17		0	3	
1891	December	28		0	3	
1892	October	1	L	3	2	
1893	January	30		1	2	
1893	February	18		3	2	
1893	April	29		4	1	
1893	December	9	L	4	3	
1893	December	30	L	4	2	
1894	April		U. C. L	0	3	
1894	April		U. C. L	0	4	
1894	September	8	L	2	4	
1894	November	3	L	2	1	
1895	March	9	U. C. L	2	0	
1895	April	16	U. C. L	2	3	
1895	October	5	L	2	5	
1896	December	7	L	0	4	
1896	September	5	L	1	1	
1896	October	3	L	1	1	*
1896	November	18	L	1	2	
1897	October	30	L	3	4	
1897	December	18		4	2	
1898	April	11	L	0	5	

*Game abandoned 20 minutes before time.

CUP GAMES

YEAR	DATE					
1892	March	9	v	West Brom	2 - 6	
1893	January	21	v	Casuals	4 – 0	
1893	February	4	v	Everton	2 - 4	
1894	January	27	v	Heanor	1 – 0	
1894	February	10	v	Middlesboro	2 – 0	
1894	February	24	v	Notts	1 - 1	
1894	March	3	v	Notts	1 - 4	Replay
1895	February	2	v	Southampton	4 – 1	
1895	February	16	v	Liverpool	2 – 0	
1895	March	2	v	Aston - Villa	2 – 6	
1896	February	1	v	Everton	0 – 2	
1897	January	30	v	Sheffield Wednesday	1 – 0	
1897	February	18	v	Sunderland	3 – 1	
1897	February	27	v	Liverpool	1 – 1	
1897	March	3	v	Liverpool	0 - 1	Replay
1898	January	29	v	Grimsby	4 – 0	
1898	February	13	v	Gainsboro Tr	4 – 0	
1898	February	26	v	West Brom	3 – 2	
1898	March	19	v	Southampton	1 - 1	Semi-final
1898	March	24	v	Southampton	2 - 0	Replay
1898	April	16	v	Derby County	3 - 1	Final – **English Cup Won**

NOTTS FOREST CUP HISTORY

1883 – 84	Scratched	To Redcar			1st Round
1884 – 85		Queens Park	1 - 1		
1884 – 85		Queens Park	3 - 1	Replay - Lost	
1885 – 86		Stavely	2 - 1	Lost	3rd Round
1886 - 87		Lockwood Bros.			3rd Round
1887 - 88		Sheffield Wednesday			5th Round
1888 - 90		Chatham (after 2 draws)			2nd Round
1890 - 91		Derby Midland			1st Round
1891 - 92		Sunderland			3rd Round
1892 - 93		Everton			2nd Round

RECORD OF MATCHES PLAYED BY FOREST FOR THE CUP

1878	November	16	v	Notts County	3-1
1878	December	21	v	Sheffield	2-0
1879	January	28	v	Old Harrovians	2-0
1879	February	25	v	Oxford United	2-1
1879			v	Old Etonians	1-2 Semi-final
1879	November	8	v	Notts County	4-0
1879	December	13	v	Turton	6-0
1880	January	31	v	Blackburn Rovers	6-0
1880	February	19	v	Sheffield	2-2
Forest were subsequently awarded a bye as Sheffield declined to play extra time					
1880	March	27	v	Oxford United	0-1 Semi-final
1880	W. O . Caius College scratched				
1880	December	4	v	Aston Villa	1-2
1881	November		v	Aston Villa	?
1882	W. O. Forest, Brigg scratched				
1882	December	2	v	Sheffield Healey	7-2
1883	January	6	v	Sheffield Wednesday	2-2
1883	January	13	v	Sheffield Wednesday	2-3 Replay
1883	Forest W. O. Redcar and Coatham scratched				
1883	December	1	v	Notts County	0-3
1884	November	8	v	Rotherham	5-0
1884	December	6	v	Sheffield Healey	4-1
1885	January	3	v	Sheffield Wednesday	2-1
1885	January	24	v	Notts Swifts	1-0
1885	February	21	v	Old Etonians	2-0
1885	March	14	v	Queens Park	1-1 Semi-final
1885	March	28	v	Queens Park	0-3 Replay
1885	October	31	v	Mellors Ltd	6-2
1885	November	21	v	Notts Olympic	4-1
1885	December	5	v	Stavely	1-2
1886	October	30	v	Notts Olympic	3-0
1886	November	13	v	Grimsby	2-0
1886	November	20	v	Grimsby	1-0 Replay
1886	December	11	v	Lockwood Bros.	1-2
1887	October	15	v	Notts Swifts	2-1
1887	November	7	v	Mellors Ltd	2-0
1887	November	28	v	Notts County	2-1
1887	December	17	v	Old Etonians	6-0
1888	January	7	v	Sheffield Wednesday	2-4
1889	February	2	Lingfield Athletic scratched the day before. Played a friendly which they won 3-1			
1889	February	2	v	Chatham	1-1
1889	February	16	v	Chatham	2-2 Replay
1889	February	29	v	Chatham	2-3 2nd Replay
1890	January	18	v	Derby Midland	0-3
1891	January	17	v	Clapton	14-0
1891	January	31	v	Sunderland Albion	1-1
1891	February	7	v	Sunderland Albion	3-3 Replay
1891	February	11	v	Sunderland	0-4

1892	January	10	v	Newcastle East End	2-1
1892	January	13	v	Sunderland Albion	1-0
1892	February	13	v	Preston North End	2-0
1892	February	27	v	West Brom	1-1 Semi-final
1892	March	4	v	West Brom	1-1 Semi-final Replay
1892	March	9	v	West Brom	2-6 Semi-final Replay
1893	January	21	v	Casuals	4-0
1893	February	4	v	Everton	2-4
1894	January	27	v	Heanor	1-0
1894	February	10	v	Middlesbrough	2-0
1894	February	24	v	Notts County	1-1
1894	March	3	v	Notts County	1-4 Replay
1895	February	2	v	Southampton	4-1
1895	February	6	v	Liverpool	2-0
1895	March	2	v	Aston Villa	2-6
1896	February	1	v	Everton	0-2
1897	January	30	v	Sheffield Wednesday	1-0
1897	February	18	v	Sunderland	3-1
1897	February	27	v	Liverpool	1-1
1897	March	3	v	Liverpool	0-1 Replay
1898	January	29	v	Grimsby	4-0
1898	February	13	v	Gainsboro Trinity	4-0
1898	February	26	v	West Brom	3-2
1898	March	19	v	Southampton	1-1 Semi-final
1898	March	24	v	Southampton	2-0 Semi- final Replay

FINAL.

Record Crowd at the Crystal Palace.

The Reds Astonish the Football World.

A DREAM OF DERBY COUNTY AND THE ENGLISH CUP

Here's to Derby's famous team
Who throughout the world are known
Better lads could not be seen
True football they have shown
For lovers of the grand old game
Will surely, by your action
Say they've not lost their fame
But gives satisfaction
There's good old Johnny, bless his name
We are ever proud to own hi
With Archie Cox and Turner too
Who play a sterling game
Methven and Leiper, two good full-backs
Who'll never lose ther name
There's Boag, Stevenson and McQuuen
They play a pretty game
And Steve Bloomer, we all know
O'er England's made a name
So lets wish them all good luck
And that by their sterling play
They win the England Cup

Boots and Shinpads

A DREAM OF DERBY COUNTY AND THE ENGLISH CUP

Last night as I lay in my little bed
So warm and so snug, with the clothes o'er my head
I had a dream that I was in London town
Making my way to the Palace ground
To see a football team
I pushed along through a maddening crowd
Some singing, some whistling, some shouting aloud
I saw in the distance a field so grand
On the side of that field a palace did stand
I heard such a shout that rent the air
It seemed as though there were millions there
I got on the field, it was such a sight
There I saw the lads dressed in black and white
I fancied I saw another team there
But who that team was I could not swear
I fancied I saw old Johnny Goodall
Taking his men down the field with the ball
All at once a shout went up
Someone shouted we've won the cup
For the County had scored, goal number one
It was all over - the fight, it was done
The other team tried hard to avert defeat
But the County has got them, they held them a sweet
I fancies I heard the whistle blow
Back again, to Derby of course we must go
I made my way back to the station
For the news would soon be spread o'er the nation
I thought at last the task was done
For the County – the English cup has won.

SINGING THE PRAISES OF THE DERBY TEAM.

They left the field favourites of everyone, except some of the disappointed Derby trippers.

The Reds commenced to show sterling football in the first few minutes of the game, and they kept it up right away to the interval.

A DREAM OF DERBY COUNTY AND THE ENGLISH CUP

Our men they been fighting
For the English Cup
They have bravely done their duty
And never once gave up
With the teams they have had to meet
Although it looked some weeks ago
That we should have defeat
Our men have been determined
To try what they could do
And their determination
Has pulled the County through
Many thousands of supporters
Came from far and wide
To cheer the good old County
And honour them with pride
We anxiously are waiting
Till the final day shall come
And if our men will do their best
We'll have the cup at home
When thousands of supporters
At the station will be up
To welcome Derby County
If they win the English Cup.

Prize for the Cup winners

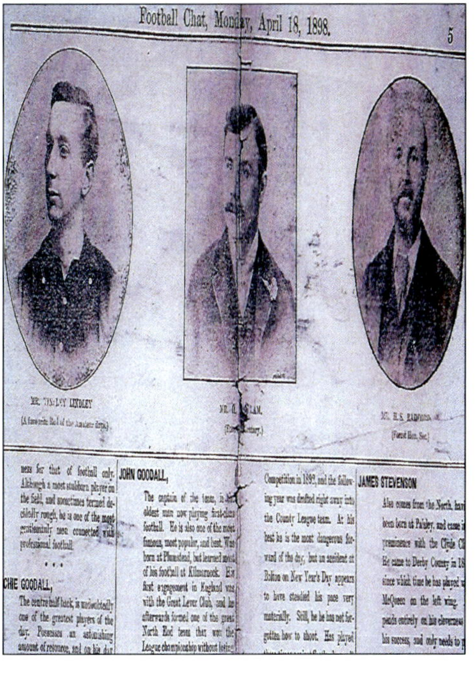

Football Chat, Monday, April 18, 1898. 5

MR. TINSLEY LINDLEY
(A favourite Red of the Amateur days.)

MR. [illegible]LAM.
([illegible]ttary.)

MR. H. S. RADFORD
(Forest Hon. Sec.)

ness for that of football only. Although a most stubborn player on the field, and sometimes termed decidedly rough, he is one of the most gentlemanly men connected with professional football.

. . .

CHIE GOODALL,

The centre half back, is undoubtedly one of the greatest players of the day. Possesses an astonishing amount of resource, and on his day

JOHN GOODALL,

The captain of the team, is [illegible] oldest man now playing first-class football. He is also one of the most famous, most popular, and best. Was born at Plumstead, but learned most of his football at Kilmarnock. His first engagement in England was with the Great Lever Club, and he afterwards formed one of the great North End team that won the League championship without losing

Competition in 1893, and the following year was drafted right away into the County League team. At his best he is the most dangerous forward of the day, but an accident at Bolton on New Year's Day appears to have steadied his pace very materially. Still, he he has not forgotten how to shoot. Has played

JAMES STEVENSON

Also comes from the North, hav[ing] been born at Paisley, and came i[nto] prominence with the Clyde Cl[ub]. He came to Derby County in 18[illegible] since which time he has played [with] McQueen on the left wing. [He de]pends entirely on his cleverness [for] his success, and only needs to

THE ENGLISH CUP, 16 APRIL 1898,NOTTM FOREST V DERBY COUNTY

In the year of 1898
History will go down
When our Nottingham Forest
Thrashed poor old Derby Town

It was on the ground of the Palace
Down in London Town
In front of 62,000
A record cheering crowd

It was in the 19th minute
That Arthur Capes, he started the score
But on the stroke of 35
Derby's Bloomer got one more

With the score at evens stevens
Forest looked forlorn
Until captain John McPherson
Shouted let's get more

The Forest they responded
They pushed, and pushed, and pushed
But Fryer saving well enough
Could not stop Arthur Capes shot

A second goal for the Forest
On the minute of 48
Going in at half-time
The crowd thought it was great

Of the restart of the final
Derby, how they pressed
Corner after corner
They really done their best

It was in the 84th minute
A corner Forest did get
The ball coming out to McPherson
Sealed Derby County's fate

That third goal on 85
The captain he did score
All the Forest fans were standing up
Shouting "We have won the Cup"

Then back to Nottingham Forest went
So happy and so proud
To wave the trophy in the air
To cheering waiting crowds

Ron Clarke

THE ENGLISH CUP FINAL
APRIL 16th, 1898 KICK-OFF 3.30pm ATTENDANCE: 62,000
DERBY COUNTY v NOTTINGHAM FOREST

For those who like to reckon up forms by the doings of the teams this season we append the records of the clubs in summary form divided into league games, club matches and club ties, a comparison show Nottingham Forest to be much the superior team to Derby County, but outside Nottingham it would be difficult to find many followers of the game who would back Nottingham Forest for a win or even a draw, taking first the league doings of the clubs it is seen that out of 29 matches Forest and Derby have only been able to squeeze 25 goals, in the matter of scoring Forest have the advantage, for they have a credit balance of 4 goals against a debit of 6 goals, as follows to Derby County, who on Saturday has been beaten by 5 goals to nil by Preston North End and 3 to nil on Monday.

Tinsley Lindley
Aged 17 at Cambridge

THE ENGLISH CUP 1898 (INCOME)

Derby County	v	Aston Villa	1,014	9	0
Sunderland	v	Sheffield Wed.	824	0	0
Everton	v	Blackburn Rovers	686	0	0
Notts County	v	Wolves	500	17	0
West Brom	v	New Brighton	375	0	0
Sheffield Utd.	v	Burslem P.V.	74	14	0
Southampton	v	Leicester Fosse	326	3	0
Nottingham Forest	v	Grimsby Town	300	0	0
Luton Town	v	Bolton Wanderers	270	17	0
Bury	v	Stoke City	233	5	0
Burnley	v	Woolwich Arsenal	156	0	0
Man. City	v	Wigan	137	0	0
Preston North End	v	Newcastle	126	2	0
Newton Heath	v	Walsall	124	4	0
Long Eaton	v	Gainsboro Trinity	52	2	0
Liverpool	v	Hucknall	38	0	0
Burslem P.V.	v	Sheff Utd (replay)	52	0	0
		TOTAL	**5,890**	**0**	**0**

THE ENGLISH CUP 2nd ROUND

Wolves	v	Derby County	667	12	0
Stoke	v	Everton	663	0	0
West Brom	v	Sheff Wed.	581	18	6
Southampton	v	Newcastle	417	17	0
Burnley	v	Burslem P.V.	328	19	6
Bolton W.	v	Man. City	325	19	6
Newton Heath	v	Liverpool	289	0	0
Nottingham Forest	v	Gainsboro Trinity	274	0	0
Liverpool	v	Newton Heath (replay)	150	0	0
Everton	v	Stoke (replay)	56	0	0
		TOTAL	**4,077**	**7**	**0**

THE ENGLISH CUP 3rd ROUND

Bolton W.	v	Southampton	207	0	0
West Brom	v	Nottingham Forest	594	0	0
Derby County	v	Liverpool	528	0	0
Burnley	v	Everton	794	0	0

3rd ROUND REPLAYS

Southampton	v	Bolton Wand.	531	0	0
Liverpool	v	Derby County	421	0	0

THE ENGLISH CUP SEMI-FINAL

Nottingham Forest	v	Southampton	839	1	6
Derby County	v	Everton	922	0	0
		TOTAL	**1,815**	**1**	**6**
		GRAND TOTAL	**14,813**	**18**	**6**

THE CUP AGAIN COMES TO NOTTINGHAM
NOTTS FORESTERS v DERBY RAMS
CUP FINAL RECORD AT CRYSTAL PALACE Attendance: 62,000

Nottingham Forest	v	Southampton	839	1	6
Derby County	v	Everton	922	0	0
		TOTAL	**1,815**	**1**	**6**
		GRAND TOTAL	**14,813**	**18**	**6**

"THE REDS ASTONISH THE FOOTBALL WORLD"

"GLORIOUS VICTORY FOR THE REDS"

"THE CUP COMES TO NOTTINGHAM FOR THE 2nd TIME"

On Saturday, Nottingham and Derby lovers of football had an opportunity of witnessing 2 of their favourite teams compete in the final of the English Cup at Crystal Palace, London, never in the history of Derby County club have their thousands of sturdy loyal supporters had an opportunity of seeing their club represented in the final of the cup, either at London, or elsewhere, but this can hardly be said of the Nottingham enthusiasts.

AT THE MIDLAND STATION

Owing to the fact that all reporters are early birds, we can only give our impressions of the palatial buildings in station street, owned by the midland company, even as early as 5am. The station presented a fairly animated appearance, sleepy eyed looking mortals with cherry red ties come marching in, and after a re-assuring glance at the magnificent clock of which the station boasts, and a comparison with their own tickets, they proceeded with commendable unanimity to visit the refreshment room, in the word of the evening post placards, we saw a "desperate raid on the buffet - great slaughter of buns".

Having swelled the revenue of the company in this particular department I sympathised with the waitresses at having to rise at such an unholy hour, and won their good graces, we took possession of the carriage reserved for us in the 6am train by Mr. Will Scaimon "Good Old Bill Adams" (whom we must not forget on his smartness and completeness of his arrangements), and after a journey more remarkable for safety than speed found ourselves at St. Pancras ready for breakfast and the final needless to say, the exodus from Nottingham was tremendous and one could not help fancying, that before midday the city would be deadly dull as well, say the Herculaneum after an historic eruption.

ARRIVAL IN LONDON

Just before reaching St. Pancras, there were many evidences of football fever, even the railway servants got it most violent, one so badly that he was holding up a piece of board with the following description.

Forest 5 v Derby 1

One man in charge of a shunting engine was evidently of a different opinion for on his engine he had chalked in very bold letters.

Derby 2 v Nottingham Forest 1

Along Euston Road there were many signs of football lovers, for club colours were to be on all sides, and vendors of black and white button hole cord appeared to be doing a thriving business, many of the London enthusiasts buying magpie colours, for no other reason than to be smart and up-to-date with the favourite colours.

At a very early hour of the day, the evening papers made their appearance, in either team the goalkeepers are capable, the backs sound, the halves useful, and the forwards clever, Derby are, perhaps a little faster forward, the Forest on the other hand, will have in their rear, 3 defenders who have long been accustomed to combine. Fryer the Derby goalkeeper is the tallest footballer in the league, he is a worthy successor to Robinson the international, he will have before him a desperate left back in Leiper a sure kick and a subtle tackler, while Methven at right back is not to be despised, as truimvirate, these players are perhaps not so solid as Allsop, Ritchie and Scott are renowned for their coolness in the mouth of goal and unlimited resources, these attributes will doubtless be brought into play, for the Derby forwards are a tricky speedy quintet, the only English men on the line are Bloomer and John Goodhall on the right wing, the veteran is on the slow side, especially for a touchline position, but the pair work together with such sublime artistry that they are sure to demand considerable attention, in the middle of the season it was said that Bloomer would never play football again, his success in the international at Celtic Park and in other matches during the past few weeks shows that Bloomer is still a power on the field, as a shot he is as dangerous as any man in the league, he scored 2 goals against Scotland and occupies a high place among league scores, which is more surprising when one considers his long absence from the game, like Fryer the goalkeeper, Boag the centre forward is without experience for the best part of the season, Derby depended on McConnachie who was transferred to Notts County, Boag has assured his place as successor, has has scored a large number of goals, and has cleverly adapted his style to requirements.

The left wing pair is a Scottish partnership and centres very finely, Stevenson is not so certain a player, but on his best day has few superiors, as the spectators came along in groups passing the time away most pleasantly, the crowd assembled very rapidly and from 8 or 9000 at 1.30, it had increased to at least 30.000 at 2.30 and another 20.000 by 3pm.

A fine band gave a capital selection of music at the centre of the ground, and concluded their programme with the national anthem about 3.10.

A grand blend of colour was lent to the crowd by the large assembly of soldiers, whose variety of dress was particularly pleasing to the eye, flags representing the colours of the two clubs were bravely floated amongst the seething mass on the popular sides of the ground and evoked torrents of applause from the friends of the rival side, "Forest" were the first to the field and received a flattering reception, but it did not equal the one given by the "County" the Londoner's joining their applause with that of the Derby trippers.

The much talked about demonstration against the "Forest" and the referee, Mr. Lewis did not come off, the southerners evidently thinking it wise not to show such childish and absurd conduct, had they done so there would probably have been many years without an association final, for the council would have been compelled to take very serious action against any organised demonstration against a team or one of their officials.

MATCH KICK-OFF 3.30pm

Johnny McPherson won the toss and Boag kicked off, the ball was returned to Forest, but Benbow was given off-side amidst loud boos from the spectators, the Forest got a free-kick, then the game was stopped due to J. Goodhall being injured, the ref, restarted by throwing the ball up, Capes forced a corner, Fryer gave Forest a 2nd corner, but Derby were given a free kick by McInnes for pushing, then McQueen who was assiduously fed by his comrades was seen careering along in a promising style, when Ritchie passed him unfairly, but Forman cleared the free kick with a fine overhead kick, and where Johnny Goodall immediately afterwards looked very dangerous, Wragg who had evidently sustained an injury in this previous collision with Stevenson proved equal to the occasion as a series of throws on the County left was followed by desultory pair in their half, until Methven after heading away a fine shot by McInnes was forced by the same forward to concede a corner, this was not improved upon by the Forest, nor was a succeeding one, and from the latter John Goodall got away and obtained a similar advantage on his side, owing to Wragg's inability to cope with him, nothing however came of the corner kick, and McInnes spoiled a likely run by placing the ball too far forward thus enabling Fryer to clear, Scott returned the leather by a beautifully judged kick and Benbow passing to Richards, the latter netted the ball, but the whistle had gone for off-side against the Forest centre, a very doubtful decision, a judicious pass by McInnes to his partner led to a warm attack on the county citadel and the reds experienced a bit of hard luck, whilst Fryer had difficulty in disposing of a long shot by Ritchie, a nasty charge in the back by Leiper on Benbow resulted in a stoppage of the game, whilst the Forester recovered, the ref, not awarding a free-kick for the foul, after the ball was thrown up, McQueen darted away and beating Forman, was pushed by the latter, the advantage of the free-kick "Capes" scored after 19 minutes of play amidst loud cheering, encouraged by his success, the reds went at it with even more vigour and Ritchie and Scott were both loudly applauded for fine kicking indeed, the Forest backs were playing a splendid game and Allsop, rarely troubled, he had however to rush out and catch a centre from McQueen, following Spouncer, changed the venue, but finalised by shooting over.

A dangerous attack in which the whole of the Derby forwards particularly were frustrated by a beautiful overhead kick, and from a fine clearance a free-kick from Spouncer near the touchline sent in a fine shot into Fryers arms, McQueen was going great guns, his runs along the touchline and accurate centres continually threatening danger to the Forest stronghold, though Ritchie was holding him in check well, on one occasion being loudly applauded for robbing him, Benbow after a game struggle with Archie Goodall and Methven, had hard lines with a fine shot which skimmed over the bar as he was grassed, following a bit of tricky work by McQueen, Allsop was called upon to punch away a long, shot, being at the same time unfairly charged into the net, the referee not noticing this infringement. The county then had hard lines owing to a fine shot striking Scott's back and still keeping up the attack, Bloomer gained a corner which the reds safely negotiated, Archie Goodall being penalised for pushing Forman in the back as he was about to shoot, and the relief came to the county through a foul by Forman for pushing McQueen this was clear infringement and from the free-kick Bloomer jumped up and headed the ball into the net, the equalising goal coming at the end of 35 minutes of play, the Forest captain could now be heard exhorting his men to keep their heads and the reds rushed down towards Fryer who had to leave his goal hurriedly to kick away. McInnes netted the ball from a free-kick given against Archie Goodall for tripping McInnes, but no other player had touched the ball from the free-kick, McQueen darted away and sent in a splendid centre which Scott headed away in equally fine style, whilst after the same forward completely beat Ritchie, he sent in another dangerous centre which Scott disposed of by rushing across and kicking it out, after Forman had been penalised for a foul throw McQueen got away again and Forman could only stop him by kicking out, fine play by the Forest left wing resulted in Turner being made the subject of a "Ludicrous" foul but the county fortunately did not suffer from this error, the free-kick being easily cleared, just on half-time Richards sent in a magnificent shot which Fryer could only beat out without caring and Capes was there to score a 2nd goal for the Forest after 48 minutes.

When the game resumed it was seen that Wragg was limping so badly as to be almost useless and Capes fell back amongst the half-backs, Wragg playing, or attempting to play outside Spouncer, McInnes was first prominent for the reds having a shot from near the touchline, which Leiper appeared to touch behind, though a goal-kick was given, the Forest outside right had another try from the same position, but his shot travelled past the post at a great rate, Forman was now limping badly and indeed it was evident that not a few players were beginning to feel the effects of their hard knocks, Derby were taking the advantage of the defensive tactics of the reds and were continually on the aggressive, Bloomer on one occasion seeming ready to score, but sending a swift shot just outside the post whilst later on a promising attack was thrown away by McQueen, beating the ball down with his hand still keeping up the pace the Derby men came again, only for Stevenson, when he looked all over to score, headed just past the upright, then the Forest retaliated, but Benbow passing to Spouncer sent the ball too far forward, the latter however gained possession, after a brilliant run in which he beat Methven he centred beautifully at full speed, Fryer cleverly punching away with several opponents around him, immediately after he looked quite beaten, he disposed of another wicked shot, the County however soon rallied and play raged around Allsop, until Scott cleared with a big kick, another assault was made, but from a corner kick taken by Goodall, Leiper got the ball and Richards robbing him, tried to struggle through, Methven coming to the rescue after Spouncer had again troubles Fryer, Allsop cleared smartly during a scrimmage and brought another fine save at the cost of a corner, this was not turned to any advantage and Benbow aroused tremendous applause by a plucky struggle with Methven, whom he completely beat, the back being only able to stop the little centre by tripping him, from a free-kick the Derby goal had a lucky escape, and a lovely shot from McInnes must surely have taken effect had it not struck the heels of Benbow, who was sprawling on the ground, a free-kick for a foul by Bloomer on McPherson was not turned into account and from one against A. Goodall close to the Derby goal, the ball, shot behind, a mis-kick from Forman nearly resulted in Derby obtaining a corner, but Ritchie saved well in the nick of time and from the resulting throw-in Boag shot behind.

Following a free-kick against McPherson, Capes saved an awkward situation by conceding a corner and from this the Forest goal had a very narrow escape and the ball suddenly out of scrimmage and just shaved the outside of the upright, Derby were striving in heroic fashion against the adverse odds and things looked ominous for the Forest when a mistake by Scott, really the first he had made, let in the County right wing, but Goodall made a mess of the opening sending the ball right to McPherson, at another time Boag appeared certain to score, but the ball cannoned off Forman, another remarkable decision on the part of the referee envoked mingled wrath and amusement, Spouncer after taking the ball himself three parts down the length of the field, being given off-side as he was about to shoot, Boag nearly got through and the Forest goal only escaped by reason of a mixture of good luck and goalkeeping, whilst Bloomer spoiled another likely goal by laying off-side, after a few minutes of play of a scrambling kind Methven was applauded for prettily disposing Spouncer, but Wragg was several times the recipient of less pleasant attentions for kicking out when hard pressed, undoubtedly the poorer thing to do having regard to his lameness, from a free-kick Allsop kept out a header from J. Goodall and the ball falling at Stevenson's feet, he had an opening, but apparently lost his head and shot wildly, it now wanted but 4 minutes to time and the crowd was already beginning to break into the piece, just as each side straining every muscle, the Forest gained a corner and the ball coming out to McPherson, who was about 20 yards away from goal, he returned it with a lightening shot which passed just under the bar, Fryer hardly seeing the ball until it was laying in the net,

3-1 to the Forest, time called, "Cup Won"., which was taken back to the Forest H.Q. at the Maypole Yard, Nottingham.

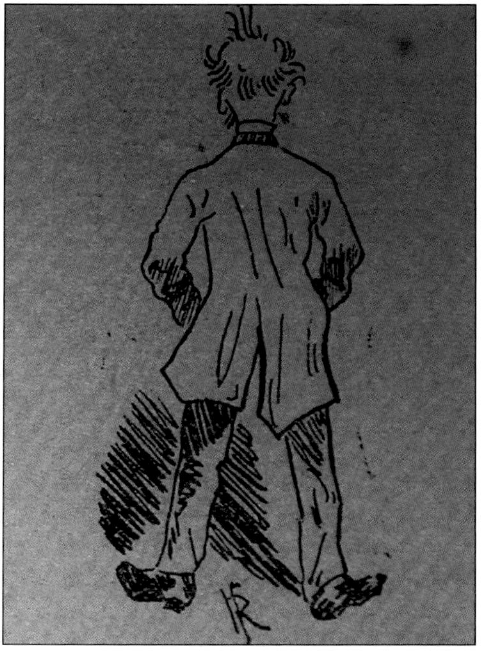

THE CUP FINAL APRIL 16th 1898
NOTTINGHAM FOREST v DERBY RAMS
KICK-OFF 3.30pm ATTENDANCE: 62,000

MINUTE BY MINUTE OF THE MATCH

3.29 McPherson won the toss

3.30 Boag kicked officiating

3.31 Benbow given off-side

3.32 Free-kick to Forest

3.33 Game stopped, J. Goodall injured

3.34 Mr. Lewis threw up the ball, Capes forced a corner

3.35 Fryer gave Forest a second corner

3.36 Derby given a free-kick on account of McInnes pushing

3.37 McInnes forced another corner, followed by a 2nd

3.38 Goodall raced away and forced a corner off Scott

3.40 Scott brilliantly robbed Bloomer

3.41 Benbow of-side, but Richards shot wide

3.42 Magnificent effort by Forest

4.43 Brilliant save from a great shot by Ritchie

3.44 Free-kick against Archie Goodall

3.45 Benbow injured by a nasty charge from A. Goodall

3.46 Game resumed

3.48 Free-kick, Cox holding Spouncer

3.49 Capes scores for Forest

3.50 Game resumed

3.51 Good effort by J. Goodall

3.52 Fine save by Allsop from McQueen

3.53 Spouncer shot over, when well placed

3.54 Free-kick against Cox

3.55 County shot wrong side of the Forest uprights

3.56 Grand save by Fryer from Spouncer

3.57 McQueen beaten by Forman

3.58 Fine shot over the bar by Benbow

4.00 Derby made a combined attack

4.01 Bloomer given off-side

4.02 J. Goodall forced Scott to give a corner

4.04 Free-kick given against Archie Goodall

4.05 Free-kick against Forman and Bloomer equalised

4.06 Game restarted

4.08 Allsop just saved

4.09 A. Goodall tripped McInnes, from a free-kick McInnes scored but no other player had touched the ball, not given

4.10 McQueen fairly beat Ritchie, but Scott kicked out

4.12 County shot past, but very wide

4.13 Leiper gave a corner from a centre by Spouncer

4.14 Forest take another free-kick

4.15 A series of throw-ins for Derby

4.18 Capes scores a second goal for Forest, after a fine save by Fryer

4.18 Half-time

SECOND HALF

4.26 Teams return to the field

4.27 Game resumed

4.28 McInnes forced a corner of Leiper

4.30 Forman beautifully beat Bloomer

4.31 Hands against Forest

4.32 Bloomer shot outside Forest goal

4.33 Hands against McQueen

4.34 Stevenson headed just outside

4.36 Fryer finely saved from Bloomer

4.37 Allsop saved

4.38 Hot attack on the Forest rear division

4.39 Corner to Derby

4.40 Another corner for Derby

4.42 Grand centre by Spouncer

4.43 Save by Allsop

4.44 Allsop gave a corner from Boag

4.45 Attack on the Derby goal, Fryer brilliantly saved

4.46 Bloomer pushed McPherson and gave Forest a free-kick

4.48 Bad mis-kick by Forman, but Ritchie saved

4.49 Free-kick against McPherson

4.50 Capes cleared from Bloomer

4.52 Bloomer went right outside

4.54 Bloomer tossed Scott and Forest had a free-kick

4.57 Spouncer given off-side

4.58 Forest applauded for a corner, unsuccessfully

5.00 Bloomer given off-side in Forest goal mouth

5.01 Another free-kick for Forest

5.02 Fine kicking by Adam Scott

5.04 Hands against Wragg and Derby just missed from Goodall

5.06 Spouncer made a good effort well up

5.07 Leiper gave Forest a corner and McPherson scored a 3rd goal for Forest

5.09 Corner for Derby, Forman cleared

5.10 Midfield play, and the crowd gathering in front of the pavilion

5.12 Spirited effort by Benbow

5.13 Derby sent just wide

TIME CALLED

NOTTS FORESTERS 3 v DERBY COUNTY 1

CUP WON

TAKEN BACK TO THE H.Q. AT THE MAYPOLE YARD, NOTTINGHAM

THE PLAYERS DERBY COUNTY

Name	Position	Height	Weight	Age	Born
J. S. Fryer	Goalkeeper	6.2	12-70	20	1878
J. Methven	Right Back	5.8	12-20	28	1870
J. Leiper	Left Back	5.8	11-11	24	1874
J. D. Cox	Right Half	5.7	11-30	28	1870
A. Goodall	Centre Half	5.6	12-20	32	1866
J, Turner	Left Half	5.11	12-90	28	1870
J. Goodall	Outside Right	5.9	12-00	35	1863
S. Bloomer	Inside Right	5.8	11-30	24	1874
J. Boag	Centre Forward	5.9	11-60	22	1876
J. Stevenson	Inside Left	5.6	11-11	22	1876
H. McQueen	Outside Left	5.7	11-60	27	1871
J. Stanley	Reserve Back	5.6	11-60	28	1870

SPENCER FRYER

The goalkeeper, born at Cromford, Derbyshire and is one of the tallest custodians in England, he has risen to his present position very rapidly, as a year ago he was keeping goal for the village club in Cromford, he is good at all sports and also good at shots and for a youngster keeps his head very well.

In addition to being a good goalkeeper he is a useful wicket-keeper, in which capacity he plays for the Indcoope and Company Brewery at Burton-on-Trent.

J. METHVEN

The right full-back, he was born in Perth Scotland and has played his football ever since hew could kick a ball, as a youth of 14, he was drafted into the Norton Park Club, Edinburgh, and 4 years later joined the St. Bernard's Club, he has played for Derby County since 1891 and has established his reputation as a sure tackler, a strong kick, very cool and never gets flurried.

J. LEIPER

The left full-back, he is a player of a slightly different stamp to his partner, exhibiting more dash and speed, he can kick well in all positions, he was born at Partick, Glasgow and learned his football with the Minerva Club at Glasgow, after playing at junior international level, he came to Derby County in 1892 and won a permanent place in the league side early the following year.

J. D. COX

The clever right half-back of Derby County, he was born at Spondon, a village a few miles outside Derby, the first team of any importance that he played with was Long Eaton Rangers about 8 years ago, a year later he signed for Derby County and commenced playing at outside left but later went to right-half, a position which he has occupied with great distinction ever since, in his first year in that position he gained his Irish cap, and it was very possible that for his recent injury he might have had more, although a stubborn player on the field and sometimes termed decidedly rough, he is one of the most gentlemanly men connected with professional football.

ARCHIE GOODALL

The centre half-back is undoubtedly one of the greatest players of the day, he possesses an astonishing amount of resource and on his day honestly does the work of two ordinary men, he was born in Ireland , a fact that the Irish authorities have persistently ignored in selecting their international teams, he has played for Kilmarnock, Liverpool, Stanley, Aston Villa, Preston-North-End and Derby County, he threw in his lot with the last named club in 1889-18990, and rendered them a splendid service as full-back, half-back and centre forward, in either of which positions he is equally at home.

J. TURNER

He hails from the neighbouring county of Staffordshire, having first seen the light at the Black Bull in the Potteries, a series of good performances on behalf of local clubs proved a stepping stone to better things and a season or two with them he went to Stoke, at the commencement of the season of 1896-1897 Derby County secured him. He is a good bustling player and generally at home on heavy ground and this year was a member of the English team that defeated Ireland at Belfast.

J. GOODALL

He has played most of his football at Kilmarnock, his first engagement in England was with the Great Lever Club and afterwards formed one of the North-End teams that won the League Championship without losing a goal, he joined Derby County in 1889-1890 and has been a tower of strength to them in various ways, he has played for England on 14 occasions and is a popular man wherever he goes, though the proprietor of an hotel. John like his brother Archie is a tea-total and non smoker.

STEPHEN BLOOMER

He was born at Cradley Heath in the black country, but spent most of his life in Derby. He won his spurs in a boys shield competition in 1892 and the following year was drafted right away into the country league team, at his best, he is the most dangerous forward of the day, but an accident at Bolton on new years day, appears to have steadied his pace very materially, still he has not forgotten how to shoot, he has played 3 times against Scotland as well as against Wales and Ireland.

J. BOAG

The centre forward, born in Glasgow and came to Derby County from East Stirlingshire club 2 years ago, he had a trial with the present league club at the commencement of the present season, but was dropped, only to be re-introduced when McConnachies ineligibility was discovered, he is a useful player and can shoot at goal.

J. STEVENSON

Also comes from the North, having been born in Paisley, he came to Derby in 1895, since that time he has played with McQueen on the left-wing he depends entirely on his cleverness for his success and only needs to part with the ball a little more promptly to become one of the finest forwards of the day.

HUGH McQUEEN

He was born in Lanark, Scotland and after serving an apprenticeship with Leigh Athletic, joined the Liverpool club and being transferred to Derby County in 1895, he and Stevenson made a very powerful wing, McQueen's centres are a great feature of his play and many goals have been scored from them.

J. STANLEY

The reserve full-back was born at Newhall, Derbyshire and came to prominence with the Derby Midland club, when that club was disbanded in 1881. He joined Derby County and has repeatedly played for the league team with great success, he is a capital back and possessed with plenty of pluck and dash.

THE PLAYERS OF NOTTINGHAM FOREST

Name	Position	Height	Weight	Age	Born
D. Allsop	Goalkeeper	5.10	12-20	27	1871
A. Ritchie	Right Back	57	12-00	27	1871
A. Scott	Left Back	5.5	12-70	27	1871
F. Forman	Right Half	5.11	12.10	22	1876
W. Wragg	Left Half	5.11	12-30	22	1876
J. McPherson	Centre Half	5.8	11.70	30	1868
T. McInnes	Outside Right	5.8	13-00	24	1874
C. Richards	Inside Right	5.6	11-11	22	1871
L. Benbow	Centre Forward	5.6	10-80	23	1875
A. Capes	Inside Left	5.8	12-80	23	1875
A. Spouncer	Outside Left	5.9	9-11	20	1878

D. ALLSOP

An excellent goalkeeper and an essay in serious football was made with the club of the town known as Leys Recreation, two years later he found his way into the Derby Junction eleven, at that time in the Midland League and for whom he played during 3 seasons, when however in 1892-1893 the Forest were admitted to the league he was induced to transfer his services to the reds and since then has been one of the most regular members of the team, missing only a few matches, whilst not perhaps in the absolute first, his general reliability and sound judgement render him a far more reliable man than many more brilliant and daring custodians, and it is eloquent of ability between the posts that with the exception of l;last Monday's match at Derby, on only 4 occasions throughout the entire season, has he had more than 2 goals put up against him.

ARCHIE RITCHIE

He is the oldest member of the team, being among the band of Scotsmen who at about the beginning of the present decade, when professionalism was broadly recognised by the club, were imported to strengthen the team, he came to the reds from Stirlingshire for whom he played for 5 years, during which period he twice represented Stirlingshire against his native Fife and Linlithgow, besides nearing the greater distinction of getting a place in the Scottish eleven against Ireland in 1891, unassuming in method he is never the less sturdy and effective back with a good turn of speed and showing unusual discrimination, both on heading and kicking, like Allsop he was a victim to the attentions of the Southampton forwards in that memorable match at Crystal Palace, but fortunately his long rest has restored him to strength and soundness.

ADAM SCOTT

The left-back, is one of the veterans of the team, and undoubtedly the most remunerate investment the club ever made, it is now almost 8 years since he came to Nottingham from Coatbridge Albion Rovers, a comparatively unknown man, then having only gained junior honours, but it was not long before he developed those powers which have earned him the admiration of other members of the team and spectators, guilt of an act of which he has reason to be ashamed, time is leaving it's trace on his speed, he is active as ever in other respects and is still one of the finest backs playing today, his unerring judgement, his wonderful kicking powers being absolutely unimpaired, for several seasons he acted as captain, but in difference to the wishes of the departments of management who desired that the duties should be undertaken by one more closely in touch with the various departments of the team, he relinquished the position in favour of the present football year, the day that witnesses Scott's retirement from active service will be lamented, not only by those intimately associated with the club, but by all who admire a distinct ornament to the game.

FRANK FORMAN

The right half-back has long been one of the popular members of the team, but the recent honours, the highest that can be conferred upon a footballer, which have been bestowed upon him, and the manner which he has born himself under them, have served to make the supporters of the club all the more sensible of his merits, he first saw the light at Aston-on-Trent, and after playing a short time with the village team he migrated to Beeston Town, and later along with his brothers, however with the result that after a little difficulty, their transfer was granted to the Forest, modest and unassuming in private, their play is characterised by attributing not withstanding he infused into his method an enormous amount of enthusiasm and vigour, well built and comely, he is a perfect picture of the ideal young athlete on the field, and using all his advantage to excellent effect he is an awkward man to meet, he combines keen tackling and a phenomenal reach with excellent judgement in feeding his forwards, and is usually smart backing them up which often time affords him opportunities of exercising his strong capacity, last season he only just missed his cap, but this year his claims could not be overlooked and had it not been for the accident which befell him in the Irish match he would no doubt have gained triple honours.

W. WRAGG

He is another specimen of the home grown player, having been born at Lenton, Nottingham and receiving his football training with various clubs in the district, he practically made his debut with Sutton-in-Ashfield, but in the course of a few years ran the round of Notts Olympic, Newstead Byron and Hucknall Portland, from the latter of which he was with 2 or 3 seasons ago transferred to the Forest reserves, on form he has the circumvent to being speedy, quick and smart with both feet and head.

J. McPHERSON (Capt.)

The centre-half and captain of the team boasts a career in the playing field which will live with the longest and most distinguished that the game has produced, his earliest associations with football date back some 16 or 17 years when he turned out for the club of his native town of Motherwell, at centre forward in the season of 1883-1884 he joined the then powerful Cambuslang organisation for which he occasionally figured at half-back, 3 years later he was snapped up by the famous Hearts of Midlothian and it was while with them that he realised the highest ambition of a footballer, to represent his country. He first took part in 7 inter-county matches for Edinburgh and in 1890 played in the trial game for the Irish match, but lost his place in the actual encounter owing to an injury, but appears to have several more useful years ahead of him.

T. McINNES

The outside-right is the best known of the Forest forwards and undoubtedly one of the cleverest as he was one of the youngest footballers who ever crossed the border, at his best he was almost unequalled possessing as he did abnormal dribbling powers, fleetness of foot, coolness and a correct eye, in fact all the qualifications of a first class man, but this season he has played much below his form, chiefly owing to his loss of speed, and he is certainly not a McInnes of yore, he first came to England as a youth of 16, but his experience with Newcastle-East-End was not a happy one and after one season returned to the Clyde only to sign for the Forest a year later, up to this season he figured on the outside left, but he is equally at home on either wing, he took his benefit game a short time ago and realised the best ever accorded to a footballer in Nottingham.

CHARLES RICHARDS

He is a native of Burton-on-Trent who chiefly learn't his football in Nottingham and the countryside, he first appeared with Newstead Byron from whom he went to Notts County, but doing nothing startling he dropped back into comparative obscure football, successfully figuring with Blackwell and Greasley, the Forest authorities however, discovered the innate powers within him and last season he has given commendable all round exhibition, his consistency being one of the most gratifying features of the improved attack, with Bloomer out of the way he had little difficulty in securing his Irish cap and it was an honour well deserved.

L. BENBOW

The centre forward only came to the club at the beginning of the season, but is already a great favourite with it's supporters, his loyalty and enthusiasm on the field compelling admiration, Ever since Sandy Higgins went, the centre position had been a weak spot in the attack but Benbow has pulled it together again, and once more given point and concentration to it's efforts, he not only holds his wings together cleverly but is fearless and tricky in his individual dashes and more over a shot, he is on the small side but is squarely built and possesses the heart of a giant, before coming to Nottingham he successfully operated with Oswestry Utd, Rosehill and Shrewsbury Town, he is a native of Birmingham.

ARTHUR CAPES

He was born at the Lamb Inn, Burton-on-Trent, which was kept by his father for many years, when Capes was quite a youngster his parents moved to the Bridge Inn, which adjoins the ground of Burton Wanderers, and it was about this time that Capes and his brother Adrian commenced to show much eagerness to develop into clever football players, and they were both very frequent trespassers on the ground, at which they later built up such great reputations with quite a few youngsters. Mr. W. D. Clarke (the Burton Wanderers Hon. Secretary) at the time, but now secretary of Leicester Fosse, drafted Cape into the Casuals or Wanderers 2nd team and it's here that he actually represented in Burton at the time they were signed.

ALFRED SPOUNCER

He is a Gainsboro lad, educated at the Queen Elizabeth grammer school in his native town, he commenced his football career at the age of 12 by playing for his school, nature had allotted him his proper position in the field for being left handed and left footed he once found himself in the outside left, in the season of 1893-1894, he was picked up by the Trinity Reserve, being drafted into the first team in 1895, Sheffield United had their eye on Spouncer and signed him on as a league player, but when Trinity left the Midland League for the second league, the Sheffield club gave Spouncer a free transfer to his old club, there was however an evident intention on the part of the United to secure Spouncer in view of what the Gainsboro committee considered to be danger, the leading officials of the Trinity F.C. offered terms to Spouncer to continue with them, his transfer to the Forest later was the means of helping the Trinity finances out of a little hole.

WHAT'S THIS FOREST LEADING

Instead of dancing and fiddling about with the ball, like a cat playing with a mouse, they dashed into their work with energetic efforts of great brilliancy and thoroughly surprised the big percentage of the crowd, who had predicted a great defeat for the Nottingham representatives, only a few games since the institution of the cup that has been witnessed by better football that was played magnificently and gave the county defence a terrible time, Benbow was a thorough little champion and so was Adam Scott and McPherson and in fact every player in the team, but all shall have full praise in next week's papers.

Football World.
Glorious Victory of the
Reds.
The CUP comes t

A FEW OFF-SIDE REFLECTIONS

Full details of the great match are given elsewhere, here we want to look at it only from the point of view of the governing body to whose work for the season is a fitting finale, it is in a sort of a practical demonstration of the good work done by the Football Association, quietly without fuss, the central authority carries on it's work of administration, wielding the immense power which is vested in it so effectively and wisely that a few of the hundreds of thousands of players whose conduct it regulates ever feel it's yoke, or realise how far reaching and irresistible it's powers are, it is only on the occurrence of some important body or person is subjected to severe penalties that the public at large get an insight into the ways and powers of the association, and it is only when one see's such an enormous gathering as there were at last year's final tie that one realises what a tremendous hold on the game it has on the public, and how great the number of these who recognise the associations authority and are bound by it's rules, it is not the last of the merits of the governing body that it controls it's vast crowd of voluntary subjects with so little friction and so little display, still further looked at from the point of view of the game as a whole the best gauges of the popularity of winter sport, no other match, not even the England v Scotland international can be regarded as furnishing anything like so accurate a test of the yearly growth of the game, to get a fair estimate, the weather must of course be propitious and a comparison of the number of people who have attended successive fine weather final ties shows a truly wonderful growth in attendance.

DERBY COUNTY 1898 CUP FINAL SIDE

Back Row Left to Right: J. Methven, A. Latham *(Trainer)*
Middle Row: J. H. Richardson, *(Secretary)* J. Fryer, J. Leiper, J. Reilly *(Director)*
Seated 2nd Row: J. Cox, A. Goodall, J. Turner
Seated Front: J. Goodall, S. Bloomer, J. Boag, J. Stevenson, H. McQueen

NOTTINGHAM FOREST ENGLISH CUP WINNERS 1898

Back Row Left to Right: Mr. H. Hallam (Secretary), F. Norman, A. Ritchie, D. Allsop, J. McPherson, W. Wragg, A. Scott, G. Bee *(Trainer)*
Front Row: T. McInnes, A. Capes, A. Spouncer

Nottingham Forest after Johnny McPherson scored the 3rd goal for Forest. This photo is the only one believed to have been taken inside the Crystal Palace ground, and was taken by Tinsley Lindley.

TINSLEY LINDLEY.

TINSLEY LINDLEYS FOOTBALL BOOTS WHICH HE PLAYED IN THROUGHOUT HIS CAREER

TOP.L.R. F.FORMAN - L.BENBOW - A.SPOUNCER.
MIDDLE, L.R. T.LINDLEY - H.HALLAM. (FOREST SEC.) - H.S.RADFORD (HON.SEC.)
BOTTOM,L.R. T. MCINNES -JOHNNY GOODALL (DERBY CAPT.) HUGH MCQUEEN.

FOOTBALL CHAT SKILL COMPETITION

No competitor succeeded in gaining the premier prize on April 2nd but no less than 22 coupons share the consolation prize of £1, we have therefore added two shillings to the prize enabling us to send each successful competitor one shilling.

The names and addresses are as follows:

Thos Belton	33 North Street, Sneinton
A. W. Streater	226 Radford Road (2 shares)
C. N. Bateman	20 Claypole Road
H. Shaw	72 Bovill Street, Radford
John Cope	5 Kingston Street, Sneinton
Stevens	212 Uttoxeter Old Road, Derby (2 shares)
Dearman	3 Eagle Place, Alfred Street Central
G. H. Vickees	13 Northumberland Terrace
F. Tyson	222 Wilford Road
W. M. Berry	11 Rock Terrace, Lower Eldon Street
F. Cope	3 North Street, Derby
J. Billesdon	18 Taylor Street, Ilkeston (2 shares)
A. A. Beck	189 Normanton Road
Herbert Toone	414 Alfreton Road
J. H. Waller	10 Wigley Street, Gordon Road
Bruce Severn	Arkwright Street (2 shares)
W. G. Tiddiman	7 Hope Drive, The Park
Harry Smith	225 Alfreton Road

For the competition on April 9th 1898, the consolation prize of £1, has been divided between the following:

W. Berry	11 Rock Terrace, Lower Elden Street
Walter Henshaw	14 Newthorpe Street
R. J. White	No address on coupon (2 shares)

Will the latter send his address in the same handwriting as his coupon (AVT).

NOTTINGHAM FOREST 1959 CUP WINNING TEAM

Back Row Left to Right: Noel Watson *(Secretary)*, Bill Whare, Joe McDonald, Booby McKinley, Roy Dwight, Chic Thomson, Jeff Whitefoot, Tommy Graham *(Trainer)*
Front Row: Johnny Quigley, Billy Gray, Jack Burkitt, Tommy Wilson, Stuart Imlach

Try HAIG'S "GLEN LEVEN," THE WHISKY OF THE WORLD.

FOOTBALL CHAT

AND CRICKET AND CYCLING RECORD.

One Penny. MONDAY, APRIL 18, 1898. One Penny.

THE CUP AGAIN COMES TO NOTTINGHAM.

THE ENGLISH CUP FINAL OF 1959

NOTTINGHAM FOREST 2 v LUTON TOWN 1

Nottingham Forest in a Cup Final
For the 3rd time
To play a team they call the Hatters
From Luton they did reside

The game was played at Wembley
North of London Town
In front of 100,000
A really colourful crowd

I was there in person
And I was only 18
Wearing a rosette for both sides
A crazy boy it seems

For I was but a neutral
But when I left that day
Seeing Forest with the cup
Really made my day

I originally come from Cambridge
And 4 years later you see
I met a girl at the Goose Fair
In 1963

We married 12 months later
And now we have a son
He supports the Forest
And thinks they are number one

We also have a daughter
Who is now just 38
I remember her little smile
When she went through the Forest gate

The little things I remember
About that Cup Final day
The ref, his name was Clough
A real famous name today

Ron Clarke

1959 CUP FINAL PROGRAMME

Nottingham Forest players and management on a visit Calverton Colliery, Thursday, September 24th 1981.
Players Unknown

In 1886 the 15th annual international match between the associations of Scotland and England was played this afternoon.

In the early days of the game the charms of the dribbling codes were rapidly recognised in Scotland and chiefly through the instrumentality of the Queens Park side, who it may be said, invented the present style of play, it became very popular here and as long ago as 1870, large crowds attended the matches played by premier clubs of Scotland, this was prior to the foundation of the Scottish association, the Queens Park early became affiliated to the English association and remains one of it's clubs to this day.

In 1872 the first international match was played between Scotland and England and so great a proficiency had been acquired by the northern dribblers that they were able to hold their own against the founders of the game, who were supposed to have been more skilful because they had more experience, the game ended in a draw, neither side scoring, the match was played in Glasgow.

When however the Scotch in the following year visited the Oval, the result was disastrous and the English won by 4 goals to 2, in 1874 Scotland began to assert superiority, which she held up to last season, when it became evident to most that the Saxon, having adopted the Scotch style of play and had become quite an expert at the game as the Scots, this is not to be regretted, as along came a string of victories gained by Scotland and it began to prove monotonous and interest engaged in the great international encounters of the season, the state of matters can readily be stated that England only won 2 matches, hence the situation of the game in 1872 at one time Scotland's superiority was strongly marked, but the tide turned contemptuously with the importation of Scotch professionals into England.

In 1874 Scotland secured it's first victory, England being beaten by 2 goals to 1, a drawn game was again played in 1875, while Scotland was in the ascendency in 1876 - 1877 and 1878, winning respectively by 3 goals to 0, 3 goals to 1 and 7 goals to 2.

The match in 1879 was a remarkable one, the Scotland team led by as many as 4 goals at half-time, in the second half of the game, which by the way was played at the Oval, the Scottish players utterly collapsed and England was not only able to equal it's opponents score, but actually turned what seemed an inevitable defeat into a triumphant victory by 5 goals to 4, in favour of the southern kingdom.

The association game had at this time risen to it's zenith, there was a plethora of first class players and in international matches, Scotland proved invincible, as a matter of fact her representatives have never since the memorable match of 1879 known defeat in a international engagement, England on the other hand has been most unfortunate, and fortune has refused to smile on her up to the present, although the majority was year by year reduced until last season, a drawn game was played at the Oval, after a splendid exibition of the dribbling code by 2 powerful teams.

The English players were not crushed by the many defeats they sustained, they put their shoulders to the wheel, and are now on a level with their great rivals, hence the games are more interesting and football of a quality which excited the feelings of the enormous crowds which assembled at Hampden Park this afternoon as showing the improvement made by England since 1880, it is only necessary to give the results of the matches played since that date, in 1881 the Saxon was against the minority, the score being 5 to 1 at Sheffield, a very exciting struggle ended in favour of Scotland by 3 goals to 2, in 1884 the last international played in Scotland, Cathkin Park being the scene of the encounter, the Scotch team won by 1 goal to 0 and in 1885 the game stood drawn 1-1.

All 14 matches that have been played, of which Scotland won 9, England 2, while 3 games have been drawn.

In all Scotland has scored 45 goals and England 24, at one time it seemed probable that no match would be played this season, but happily the dispute which threatened to cause a rupture between the two associations has been safely smoothed over, and the friendly relations re-established through good sense of the Scottish association, who following the example set by the Rugby Union, when a serious hitch kept them asunder adopted a corresponding generous spirit by the other, this matter however must now be buried in the past.

The following are the teams and their positions on the field on March 27th 1886.

SCOTLAND

M. Paton Dumbarton		W. Arnott Queens Park
J. McDonald Edinburgh	Lindsey Dumbarton	C. Campbell Queens Park
W. Grey Partshields Ath.		A. Hamilton Queens Park
Raitken Dumbarton	G. Somerville Queens Park	Sellars Battlefield

ENGLAND

Cobbold Cambridge Univ.	Lindley Nottm. Forest	G. Brann Swifts
E. Bambridge Swifts		Splisbury Cambridge Univ.
R. T. Squires Old Carthusions		J. Forrest Blackburn
P. M. Walters	H. Arthur	A. M. Walters

No fewer than 7 of the English team played in last year's international at the Oval, namely N. C. Bailey (who took part in his 9th international this afternoon, E. Bambridge, Cobbold, Forrest, Arthur and the brothers A. M. and P. M. Walters.

The following men are new to the team. Squire and Splisbury, who played against Ireland last season, and T. Lindley and Brann. The capabilities of this team were well known through the connection which the majority have wih the Corinthians, all men of proven ability, all with, perhaps the exception of Splisbury were well known to the Scotch supporters of the game, who always recognise ability, no matter where displayed, it was felt that England had made a most judicous selection of players and we are within our bounds when we say that Scotland has embarked on an international encounter with less hopes of victory.

In 1886 her representatives had found foe-men worthy of their steel and estimated these merits at their true value, the Scotch team contained 4 men new to the international honours of the highest class namely, Grey, Raitken, Summerville and McDonald.

The remainder of the eleven with perhaps the sole exception of Hamilton may be considered veterans and in the case of Campbell, he for the 10th time played against England and in this respect he stands alone as an association player, the team as a whole, while admittedly the best that could be got together did not inspire unbounded confidence, some of the Scotch players had of late been displaying rather in and out form, while others were short of work.

In 3 instances at least 3 men had not played throughtout the season, on the other hand the Englishmen were known to be all in good form, the forwards were speedy men, and that the Scotch backs would be worked hard.

INTERNATIONAL COMMENTS

It was in 1892 that England last won the international championship at both rugby and association football.

The rugby half of the double has gone off again this year, and there are only 2 more games to be played in the association tournament in which up to date the positions stand as follows:-

England	2	1	0	1	3
Ireland	2	1	0	1	3
Scotland	2	1	1	0	2
Wales	2	0	2	0	0

The remaining matches to be played are:-

England v Scotland at Glasgow

Wales v Ireland at Wales

Wales are already out of the running for the championship, but England, Scotland and Ireland all have a chance of securing it, no country is, however in a sufficiently strong position to win by it's own efforts, even if England defeat Scotland at Glasgow, she can only win the championship outright if Ireland is also beaten in Wales, Scotland's whose chance depends upon the failures of both England and Ireland, will herself have to defeat Wales and see England beaten at Glasgow, if she is to finish top, in the event of England and Ireland both proving successful in their remaining international encounters the countries will tie for the first position, with Scotland and Wales hopelessly in the rear.

THE ENGLISH TEAM CRITICISED

England have on the whole done rather well in the international matches played at Glasgow, it was at Hampden Park in 188 that an English team, which included;- W. R. Moon, T. Lindley, F. Dewhurst, J. Goodall, D. Hodgetts, J. Forrest and R. Howarth defeated Scotland by a record score of 5 goals to 0 at Ibrox.

Two years later, Scotland were beaten by 4 goals to 2 both at rugby and association football, the effect of playing in Scotland seems to have rather a stimulating effect than otherwise upon English teams.

Nine out of the players who will represent England on the 2nd of April are drawn from the 1st division of the league, the 2nd division league and the southern league, contributing one player apiece, Aston Villa, the leaders of the 1st division, have not however a single representative, the eleven men drawn are from 10 clubs, Liverpool, contributing both the goalkeeper and centre forward.

The selected team is as follows for the 2nd April 1910. S. Hardy (Liverpool), Crompton (Blackburn Rovers), Pennington (West Brom), Wedlock (Bristol City), Makepiece (Everton), Bond (Bradford City), Fleming (Swindon Town), Parkinson (Liverpool), Hardings (Sheffield), Wall (Manchester Utd) and Ducat (Woolwich Arsenal).

Six of the men who helped beat Scotland at Crystal Palace last April have been capped, the newcomers being Ducat and Makepiece in the half-back line, and Bond, Parkinson and Hardings among the forwards, of these however, only the last name is quite new to the international honours, neither the English side which drew with Ireland, nor the one which so narrowly defeated Wales at Cardiff, gave complete satisfaction, there seems to be a dearth of brilliant footballers in this country at the present time, probably due to the fact that they are not encouraged in the modern game and were it not for the fact that other countries appear to be quite as poorly off as we are, our chances of winning the international championship would be small indeed, against both Ireland and Wales our men have failed to show not only brilliance, but combination, they were selfish without being clever.

A SOUND DEFENCE

Two alterations have been made from the side that played Wales, Makepiece and Hardings taking the places of Bradshaw and Holley, Bradshaw is hardly strong enough to stop the Scottish forwards, he could not even hold the Chelsea wing in check in the players union match last Monday and Makepiece, who is a bold, resolute player and should be a decided improvement for Sunderland, Holley has been one of the most consistently successful players of the year, but he certainly does not combine well with Wall, the Manchester United outside left, but his retirement in favour of Hardings will occasion no surprise, Hardy is perhaps the soundest goalkeeper we have at the present day, although there is little in it between half a dozen that could be named fit and well, Crompton and Pennington were the obvious backs and with these 3 players the defence is not likely to let us down, neither are we to be weak at half-back with 2 workers like Wedlock and Ducat in the side, if we fail it is likely to be forward .

The reconstructed line does not look convincing on paper, Bond and Fleming make a fair wing and Parkinson if all are in form.

ASSOCIATION FOOTBALL

ENGLAND v SCOTLAND

Fortunately for the success of this, the most important association match of the year, the weather on this day was very favourable still some 12,000 spectators assembled on the park slopes.

ENGLAND v SCOTLAND MATCHES

1872	Glasgow	Draw	0-0 (1st Int. Match)
1873	Oval	England	4-2
1874	Glasgow	Scotland	2-1
1875	Oval	Draw	2-2
1876	Glasgow	Scotland	3-0
1877	Oval	Scotland	3-1
1878	Glasgow	Scotland	7-2
1879	Oval	Scotland	5-4
1880	Glasgow	Scotland	5-4
1881	Oval	Scotland	6-1
1882	Glasgow	Scotland	6-1
1883	Sheffield	Scotland	3-2
1884	Glasgow	Scotland	1-0
1885	Oval	Draw	1-1
1886	Glasgow	Draw	1-1
1887	Blackburn	Scotland	3-2
1888	Scotland	England	5-0
1889	Oval	Scotland	3-2

The final tie for the "London Charity Cup" takes place at Kennington Oval next Saturday, both clubs will be strongly represented, the holders having in their ranks, the international captain "Tinsley Lindley", who played for them when they won last year.

1890	Oval	Draw	1-1
1891	Blackburn	England	2-1
1892	Glasgow	England	4-1
1893	Oval	England	5-2
1894	Glasgow	Draw	2-2
1895	Liverpool	England	3-0
1896	Glasgow	Scotland	2-1
1897	Oval	Scotland	2-1
1898	Glasgow	England	3-1
1899	Birmingham	England	2-1
1900	Oval	Scotland	4-1
1901	Oval	Draw	2-2
1902	Birmingham	Draw	2-2
1903	Sheffield	Scotland	2-1
1904	Glasgow	England	1-0
1905	Oval	England	1-0
1906	Glasgow	Scotland	2-1
1907	Newcastle	Draw	1-1
1908	Glasgow	Draw	1-1
1909	Oval	England	2-0
1910	Glasgow	Scotland	2-0
1911	Liverpool	Draw	1-1
1912	Glasgow	Draw	1-1
1913	Oval	England	1-0
1914	Glasgow	Scotland	3-1

WAR YEARS

1919	Glasgow	England	4-3
1920	Sheffield	England	5-4
1921	Glasgow	England	3-0
1922	Birmingham	Scotland	1-0
1923	Glasgow	Draw	2-2
1924	Wembley	Draw	1-1 1st Match

DONALD GOW

Born 8th February 1868, in Blair, Scotland died? He was a Scottish footballer he played for Sunderland and the Scottish national team as a full-back.

CLUB CAREER

Previously playing for Rangers, he made his debut for Sunderland against Bolton Wanderers, September 1891 in a 4-3 defeat at Pikes Lane. Gow won the English Football League Championship while at Sunderland in 1885 and 1892. He played for Sunderland on two separate occasions, in 1891 - 1892 and 1893 - 1897 respectively, in total, making 96 league appearances scoring 1 goal in his time at Sunderland.

INTERNATIONAL CAREER

Gow made his debut for Scotland against England in March 1888 in a 5-0 defeat at Hampden Park, he had captained the Scottish side in this game, in total he made two caps for Scotland scoring no goals.

ANDREW WATSON

Queens Park, London Swifts, Corinthians and Scotland

1st black player to play in Scotland, He played for Queens Park.

Andrew Watson is wearing his London Swifts cap in this photo.

THE END

I am afraid that this is the end, I hope all the people that have read the book have had an enjoyable read.

LEONARD LINDLEY
SHERIFF OF NOTTINGHAM 1876. - MAYOR OF NOTTINGHAM 1882.
THE FATHER OF TINSLEY LINDLEY
NOTTINGHAM FOREST - CORINTHIANS - ENGLAND.

THANKS, ACKNOWLEDGEMENTS

Charlie and Olwen Lamb
Peter Holme and Phil Martin *(Preston Football Museum)*

Paul McKenna *(Former Nottm. Forest Captain)*
Cindy and Julie Clarke
Gary, Charlie and Joanne Clarke
Julian Prendergast
Sophie and Kieran MacMillan

Jo's Barbers Shop, Arnold